# A Pot of Coffee and a Resentment

# A Pot of Coffee and a Resentment

✦

## The Committee in My Head Is Now in Session

*Dana N. Sharp*

iUniverse, Inc.
New York  Lincoln  Shanghai

# A Pot of Coffee and a Resentment
## The Committee in My Head Is Now in Session

iUniverse books may be ordered through booksellers or by contacting:

iUniverse
2021 Pine Lake Road, Suite 100
Lincoln, NE 68512
www.iuniverse.com
1-800-Authors (1-800-288-4677)

The views expressed herein are the sole responsibility of the author and do not necessarily reflect the views of iUniverse or its affiliates.

ISBN-13: 978-0-595-41306-5 (pbk)
ISBN-13: 978-0-595-85661-9 (ebk)
ISBN-10: 0-595-41306-4 (pbk)
ISBN-10: 0-595-85661-6 (ebk)

Printed in the United States of America

This book is for my heroes, Mark and Tim, the most wonderful and forgiving sons a mother could have, and to my son, Trey, who chose a permanent solution to a temporary problem. Our hearts are broken but not our spirit. We love you.

... out of every season of grief or suffering, when the hand of God seemed heavy or even unjust, new lessons for living were learned, new resources of courage were uncovered, and that finally, inescapably, the conviction came that God does "move in a mysterious way His wonders to perform."

*Twelve Steps and Twelve Traditions*

This spring, a book was on the best seller's list and promoted as a memoir. I was curious as to what all the excitement was about so I downloaded the book to my ipod. I never finished the book as I had trouble believing the authenticity of some of the stories. Later the author admitted embellishing some of the facts to make the story more interesting. What you read in this book is true. Nothing is embellished; however, some names were changed out of respect for anonymity.

# Contents

# 1

## *The Beginning Years*

When I decided to write this book, the chairman of the committee in my head pounded the gavel and said, "You don't know the first thing about writing a book." "What makes you think anyone would be interested?" "Lots of people had a tougher time than you did." "One more time you think you are unique." As any alcoholic knows, this committee is always in session telling us we are not good enough, we are not smart enough, we are not handsome or pretty enough, and that we need to just sit down and feel guilty. A pot of coffee and a resentment is all the committee needs to set up chairs, bring the meeting to order, and start interrupting our thoughts.

Over the years I have been to many meetings and heard many alcoholics talk about their awful childhood and blame, blame, blame. I have many positive memories of my childhood and realize today, that it was the interpretation of events by the committee that caused my dis-ease. In this book, you will meet my family and the master of my life for twenty-one years— King Alcohol. This is not a book of blame, but simply a sharing of my life's experiences on my journey to freedom. So, let's start at the beginning.

My earliest memories revolve around the farm where my Mom lived as a child. Although we visited the farm a couple of times, I must have been around two or three years old when Mom and I lived at the farm for a short time. We were moving from Denver and Dad had gone to St. Louis to find a place for us to live. I absolutely loved this farm and still think of it often. Now, you have to remember that all these images of the farm are seen through the eyes of a three-year-old, and the memories are still in the mind of a three-year-old.

I can remember us driving the two-lane road that led to the farm, the excitement when I saw the white fence that surrounded Grandpa's land, and the rooster weather vane on the roof of the barn. When we turned on the dirt road that led up to the farmhouse, the first thing I looked for was the huge oak tree at the side of the house. Patsy, the Border collie, always ran around this tree barking when anyone approached the farm. She had run around this tree so many times that a foot deep trench was worn into the ground. After getting out of the car, I would be off to the tree to run around in the trench with Patsy, who would delight in running over and around me as I tried to keep up with her.

The farmhouse was a large, white, two story surrounded by a porch. There was no electricity, and no running water; the only light inside was from the sun during the day and the kerosene lamps at night. The main floor was a huge room with a piano in the corner. I am sure there was furniture also, but all I remember is the piano and the fireplace. The busiest part of the house was the kitchen as Grandma was always cooking something. There was a massive table in the kitchen, and since this was a working farm, she cooked breakfast and supper for the hands. We would rise with the rooster and Grandma would start frying chicken. The chickens would be gathered first thing in the morning and Grandma would tear their heads off and I watched the bodies dance all over the ground. I was fascinated by this; it never bothered me at all. The table would be overflowing with fried chicken (I always got the wishbone), freshly baked pies, biscuits, gravy, potatoes, two or three freshly picked fruits and vegetables, and lots and lots of coffee. I just can't imagine doing all this with no running water! I would be passed from hand to hand amid the laughter and conversation at the table. As the hands left for the fields I would get dozens of rough faced kisses and help Grandma clean up the kitchen as she started cooking again for supper. We would then pack up the food for the hands and take it to the fields.

My days at the farm were always full of fun things to do. There was a draft horse named Brownie and a huge pig that loved to be brushed with a corncob. Grandpa would plop me on them and lead me around the barn. On one morning, I saw that Grandpa had put Ferdinand the bull in the small fence enclosure by the barn. I promptly crawled under the wooden fence beam, and as I went to pet Ferdinand (who was not happy with my intrusion), Grandpa grabbed the back of my jumper and I flew over the fence just as the bull put his head down and started to charge. Grandpa was not mad at me; he just hugged me and told me never to do that again. And I didn't. Grandma and I would collect eggs every morning, and I hated doing this, as the hen houses smelled awful. I spent afternoons playing with kittens, chasing Patsy, and waiting for my Grandpa to come in from the field. Sometimes he came home earlier than usual and he would go shoot jackrabbits, and I would retrieve them with Patsy. We would pick gourds and Grandpa would carve pots, pans, and dishes out of them. He put wooden blocks on the pedals of the sharpening machine so I could push them to make the stone wheel go around so he could sharpen his tools.

One of my favorite things to do was to help Grandpa harness Brownie, hook up the buckboard, and go to town. I would sit next to Grandpa as he held the reins until we were out of sight of the farmhouse and then he would hand me the reins and let me lead the horse and wagon to town. What a thrill! What I didn't know at the time, was that Brownie had been to town so many times he knew the way blindfolded. I remember snow being so deep that it was like being in a long, white tunnel when we went to town. We spent evenings listening to grandma play the piano and sing, and I would chase lightening bugs with Patsy. It was a magical time at the farm, and I would cry when we had to leave.

After retiring and selling the farm, my grandparents moved to Colorado Springs. Their home was at the base of the Rockies, and every day we would hear the bells ring at the Will Rogers Shrine on Cheyenne Mountain. We would visit the Garden of the Gods, Manitu Springs and Cheyenne Mountain Zoo, and I never got tired of seeing these places. Mom would not let me ride alone in the car with Grandpa, as he was so enthusiastic about pointing things out to me she just knew he was going to drive off the side of the mountain. They didn't have guardrails back then, and there were a couple times I could hear Mom praying in the backseat. Grandpa would take me on long walks, and introduce me to everyone he knew. He loved to show me off and I loved being with him. After everyone would go to bed, Grandpa and I would meet in the kitchen and eat Ritz crackers with peanut butter. He would show me how to pack the tobacco in his pipe and how to clean his pipe. (I even had an occasional puff.) Several years after moving to Colorado, Grandpa died in his recliner from a heart attack. Grandma stayed in Colorado Springs a short time, and after living with us for a couple months, she was placed in a nursing home. Grandma was diagnosed with Alzheimers, and although she didn't know us in the end, she was perfectly happy in her own little world. She died in her sleep. I never saw my maternal grandparents take a drink of alcohol.

My paternal grandparents lived in Denver, CO. and Mom and I lived with them for a year or so when Dad was in the Navy. I was born in Denver on Thanksgiving Day, November 22, 1945, the first grandchild in the family. The story goes that my Grandpa was not happy about his turkey dinner being disrupted, and announced that he was going to finish his dinner and didn't give a damn what everybody else was going to do. My Grandpa was a strict and stern man, and I don't ever remember seeing him without a shirt and tie. He could be gruff and seldom smiled, but I just adored him. He would read me bedtime stories, some of them not quite appropriate for my age, but no one would dare suggest he read something else. He taught me one of my first songs "Cigarettes and Whiskey and Wild Wild Women" (not a top ten favorite with the rest of the family). My Grandma had a wonderful sense of humor and was always smiling. Every morning she would make breakfast for all of us and we would eat in the breakfast room. Windows surrounded the room, there was a canary in a cage in the corner of the room, and Grandpa was always telling the bird to shut up. Before every meal, my job was to roll the napkins and put them in holders for everyone. Grandma had a drawer filled with different napkin holders and she let me pick which ones we would use. I always served Grandpa breakfast (prunes and wheat toast), and he would always compliment me on what a fine job I did serving him.

I loved their house and the neighborhood; older homes with porches, alleys, ash pits and apple trees. My best friend was my Aunt, Dad's sister. Her name was Elizabeth, but since I was surrounded by uncles and could not pronounce Elizabeth, I called her Uncle Bullus. Eventually, everyone in the family started calling her Bullus. She was in college and taught me all the sorority and fraternity songs. She didn't screen the bad words and I just sang away while she doubled over in laughter. I remember her wedding to Uncle Jim and being sad that she didn't live at Grandma's any more. In later years when I would visit her and Jim, there would always be an Ella Fitzgerald record on. Their basset hound, named Poor Pitiful Pearl but called Pearlie Mae, would howl to the music. Bullus taught me how to play bridge and Jim taught me how to drive a stick shift in his little red Triumph convertible. They were so much fun to be around and I always looked forward to spending time with them. I don't remember anything about their house except for the bathroom. It was black and white marble and just the coolest room I had ever seen.

I didn't know until years later that while living in Denver I was surrounded by alcoholics. There were seven adults living at my grandparent's home and four of them were alcoholics. When I found this out it explained the behavior I witnessed as a child: my Dad throwing a shoe at me because I was making too much noise; my Dad and my Aunt Helen yelling at each other; Aunt Vi screaming at Dad; the slamming of doors; the angry faces; and my Mom crying. I have never questioned the fact that alcoholism is hereditary. I come from a long line of fine, upstanding drunks.

Grandpa died after having heart surgery in 1957 and Grandma died on October 7, 1977, the day Tim, my youngest, was born. I had called to tell her about Tim and the coroner answered the telephone. Talk about going from joy to grief. Uncle Bullus died of a brain aneurysm the day before she was due to arrive in St. Louis for my oldest son's (Trey) baptism in August of 1971. I had asked her to be Trey's godmother, and she was so eager to see and hold him. She and Jim could not have children so Trey's birth was so exciting for her. I was devastated by her death. She was still my best friend when she died. I remember I just could not stop sobbing at her funeral, and my Mom kept telling me to stop crying, I was embarrassing her. At the time of her death, I don't remember thinking about how her death affected Grandma. I was just too self-absorbed at the time, as it was all about me and how I felt.

# 2

## *Here Comes Guilt*

After living at the farm for several months, Mom and I took the train to St. Louis to be with Dad. We lived in a two-bedroom apartment in the Holly Hills area in south St. Louis. It was a nice neighborhood with lots of kids. One evening I suddenly came down with a high fever and was not able to stand. Mom called the doctor, and he came to our apartment, to see what was wrong. The doctor took me to St. Mary's Hospital for a spinal tap, and I can still remember how frightened I was. Mom pinned a St. Christopher medal on me as they took me to a room for testing. I vividly remember being hysterical and the nurses and doctors had to hold me down for the spinal tap. To this day I just panic when I lose the freedom of movement. The test showed that I had polio and I was whisked away and not allowed to see my parents. I was taken to a large room in the basement, and put in a bed in the far corner of the room. The bed had tall bars on the side so I could not get out. There was no one else in the room, and when the nurses and doctors came in, they wore masks. You can't imagine how scared I was, not knowing what was happening, and not being able to see Mom and Dad. I was in the hospital four days. I was on crutches for a short time, but came through unscathed physically. Emotionally, I was to assume guilt for getting polio as Mom said it was my fault for playing in the sprinkler. The committee in my head was gathering.

When I was seven we moved to a new apartment. All the streets were named after birds and I think ours was Bluebird Lane or something like that. I really liked this neighborhood as there were many kids and I had a little more freedom to roam. Back then parents never worried about strangers taking their kids, and I honestly think that they had never heard of the word pedophile. I went to first grade and second grade at a Catholic elementary school. It was my first introduction to nuns and I was scared to death of them. I had seen the sisters smack kids with the rosaries they wore around their waists, and crack rulers over knuckles, so I toed the line and was a perfect student out of fear not interest. I remember the first couple of weeks after starting school I cried every day when getting on the bus.

I do remember one Easter morning, as we were getting ready to go the church, my brother suddenly disappeared. Mom found him down by the creek sitting in the mud in his new white suit and white patten leather shoes. Boy was she mad! Dad and I thought it was quite funny so, true to form, Mom stopped talking to Dad so Dad would drink, and my brother and I were both to blame for what happened. One more time I felt guilty for Mom being upset; my brother could have cared less.

We packed up and moved to Skokie, IL. when I was entering third grade. We lived in a four-unit apartment building on the second floor. I absolutely loved Skokie, and still do. It was a great neighborhood to live in: lots of kids, rows of apartment buildings, alleys, walkways between buildings, gated and scary building entrances, back porches and dark, spooky basements. In the summer we would collect empty bottles at construction sites and return them for money at Harold's Bar. The bar was just a couple blocks from our apartment and every time we went into the bar to return bottles, I would see Dad inside drinking, and I knew that there would be an argument at the dinner table that night. One of our pastimes was catching gophers in milk bottles. We put our foot over one of the gopher holes, and poured water from the milk bottle into the second hole and waited for the gopher to run out and into the bottle. We would then throw the milk bottle at a rock and run like crazy, as Dad said the gopher would chase us. We would ride bikes, play football and baseball in the field across the street. I remember playing baseball one afternoon and the batter hit the ball so hard it flew into the window of the apartment next door. All the kids took off running except for me. I went over to the man who was yelling at us and apologized for breaking the window. He took down my name and address and called my Dad. Dad was furious with me. He yelled and said he could not believe how stupid I was not to run with the others. I had thought I had done the right thing, and was confused about why he was so angry. It was like the time we went to the drive-in and in the bathroom, I found a $5.00 bill. I gave the money to the manager and was so proud of myself for not keeping the money. When I told my Dad what I had done, he said he just could not believe how stupid I was and I should have kept the money. Once again, mixed signals, once again I was stupid. The one thing I did to make my Dad happy was to beat up the boy next door. His name was Art. Dad always picked on him, and I noticed that when I did the same Dad would laugh, so I began tormenting Art to get Dad's approval. I often think of Art and would like to apologize for all the times I beat him up. I started watching the *Sunday Night Fights* with Dad as that was his favorite show. Anything to get Dad's approval. The committee in my head was setting up chairs.

Dad would walk to the train station every morning to catch the *Skokie Swift* downtown. When I could, I would walk with him and then meet him at the end of the day so we could walk home together. There were times when Mom would drive to the station to pick him up because he was drunk. Dad would immediately start accusing Mom of terrible things, and she would cry telling him "Not in front of the kids." One cold and snowy evening as Dad came walking home, I was hiding behind a tree, and when he approached, I hit him in the side of his face with a snowball. Since I had been waiting awhile, smoothing the snowball to a perfect sphere, the snowball became an ice ball. It was so hard that when it hit him it didn't even break. He was livid. I will never forget the rage in his eyes. He scared me so badly I ran off and was afraid to come home. When Mom came looking for me, she said that it was OK and Dad wasn't mad. He would sit and glare at me and not speak to me for days. He never forgave me and told everyone he was hard of hearing on that side because of what I did. "Boy did you screw up this time." "No wonder they are unhappy with you." "You don't deserve to be forgiven." Fodder for the committee. It could have been worse. I could have been the one to get the beatings with the belt instead of my brother. My brother Ralph was four years younger than I was and always in trouble. He seemed to thrive on getting Dad angry, and the belt didn't seem to faze him.

I went to St. Peters School from third grade through eighth grade. The school bus would pick me up at the corner and I always looked forward to going to school. St. Peters was in the heart of town and each morning I went to Parubecks Bakery to buy orange juice and chocolate long johns to eat before going to church. I sang at Mass every morning with the choir, and on Saturdays we sang at funeral Masses. The choir loft was up a winding staircase, and I loved the smell of incense and wood polish. It was, and still is, a beautiful church. Father Sour lived up to his name, old and cranky, but we all loved Fr. Kelly, young and very good looking. In later years, we referred to Fr. Kelly as "Father What a Waste." From fourth grade through eighth grade, I was taught by nuns with good intentions, but with poor results.

It was during my school years at St. Peters that I learned about venial and mortal sins. If I didn't pull weeds in the cemetery on All Souls Day it was a mortal sin and I was going to hell. If I didn't eat all my food in the lunchroom cafeteria I had a one way ticket to hell. (I was caught stuffing sauerkraut in an empty milk carton, and Sister Columbana started praying for me right there on the spot.) In addition, those impure thoughts that Sister Arnoldine said I had were what really set my trip to hell in stone. I would dutifully confess these impure thoughts to Fr. Kelly, not having the slightest idea what they were. You would never catch me in Fr. Sour's confession line, as I was sure the penance would be early death. We decided around seventh grade that we were going to fry no matter what we did, as there was not enough time to say all the prayers (indulgences) necessary to keep us out of hell. When I snuck in the Skokie Theatre to see *Blue Denim*, my fate was sealed. In spite of all misconceptions I had regarding my soul, I was happy at St. Peters.

I was a good student, but began to feel I was not good enough. I got this message from the nuns, and from my parents. I can remember different projects I had to do for homework, such as drawing a map of the U.S. and labeling the Capitols, making valentine boxes, and tying artificial flowers for Church decorations. I would get busy with my project and upon completion proudly show it to Mom and Dad. One or the other would then say, with an undertone of disgust, "Oh, here, let me do it for you." What I heard was "Can't you ever do it right?"

Most of the kids I hung with lived within walking distance of downtown Skokie and St. Peters. We would walk to friend's homes after school and just hang out. I was the only one who lived a distance away (about three miles). My best friend Kath lived a couple blocks away and I spent a lot of time at her house. The hangout in town was Pandees. It was a hamburger place at the far end of town. We would buy cigarettes from the machine at Pandees, and we would get a booth and smoke (Kents), eat fries, and drink crème soda. It was in seventh grade that Kath and I became interested in boys. It's funny; I can still remember their names. We would spend afternoons walking past their houses as if we didn't know they lived there. We would talk to them if they happened to show up at Pandees or the Coffee Shop, but we were so nervous around them that we didn't stay long. Kath and I were totally in the dark about sex. Neither of our parents offered any information, but I knew it had to be bad because when I asked Mom what "fuck" meant she screamed at me and told me "Don't ever say that word again!" Kath had an older sister Bonnie, so we asked her to explain this sex thing. I still remember being absolutely shocked over what Bonnie said, and Kath didn't believe her and accused her of lying. We agreed it was just an awful thing to have to do, and we never talked about it again.

Some of my favorite memories are of ice skating at the small neighborhood parks. The homes surrounding the parks would drag their hoses and flood the parks so we could skate. I remember Dad buying new skates and meeting us at the park one weekend. He promptly fell flat on his face and cracked his head on the ice. After saying every bad word I ever heard, (and some I had not), he threw the skates away and cussed about this for weeks to come. Of course, it was Mom's fault for making him buy the skates, and my fault for encouraging him to try skating.

Probably the one thing I loved doing more than ice-skating was roller-skating. We would go to the Palladium every Saturday to skate. There was a room at the skating rink that had shiny, slick, linoleum tile on the floor, and a jukebox in the corner. I would come with a pocket full of quarters and dance, dance, dance. I lived for the weekend to play music and dance. I still remember the songs we danced to: "At The Hop" by Danny and the Juniors, "BeBopBaby" by Ricky Nelson, "Rockin Robin" by Bobby Day, and "Wake Up A Little Susie" by The Everly Brothers. I watched American Bandstand every day and knew all the dancers by name.

By the age of twelve the committee in my head was in full session: "It's your fault Mom cries." "It's your fault Mom and Dad fight." "It's your fault when things go wrong." "You are stupid." "You never do anything right." Dancing silenced the talking in my head, but King Alcohol was patiently waiting in the wings.

# 3

## *Another Fun Vacation*

Traveling with Mom, Dad, and my brother, was always an adventure. These trips would have made a terrific Chevy Chase Vacation movie. When we lived in St. Louis, Chicago, and moved back to St. Louis, we went to Colorado every summer to see the grandparents, and it was always a very long, very hot, miserable trip. We took the old highway 66 all the way. Back then it was a two-lane road and the speed limit was seventy miles an hour. I can remember that horrible feeling in my stomach when Dad would pass a car or truck. I was just sure that Dad was going to crash head-on as he was not a patient driver. He had a name for every driver he passed, and it started with "sonova" and then Mom would tell him to calm down. He would make some remark, and then the silence would be deafening. Mom and Dad always used the silent treatment when they were mad at you. Mom was still doing this when I was fifty-five years old! Whenever we would disagree about something, she would walk away and not speak to me for days. Infuriating.

Mom and Dad liked to drive at night when it was not so hot. It would take two and a half days to get to Colorado and it felt just as hot at night as it did during the day. Most of the motels back then didn't have air conditioning so there was seldom any relief from the heat. My brother and I were usually fighting about something: "She's looking at me." "He's on my side." and on and on. When we traveled across Kansas, there was a sign that said, "No facilities for a hundred miles." We may have gone to the bathroom five minutes before, but the minute we were a mile past this sign, my brother would have to go to the bathroom. Dad would pull over so he could go on the side of the road, and then he would not be able to pee. Back in the car, another stop in five miles, as my brother had to go, and again nothing. After the second false alarm, Dad would not pull over again, and my brother would have to hold it until Dad felt like stopping.

There was always a disaster of some kind on these trips. One time on our way home from seeing the grandparents, a golf ball shattered the windshield and Dad had to pull over so we could pick the glass out of his face and hair. On another trip, Dad ran over a skunk, and further down the road a case of mustard fell off the truck in front of us and Dad ran over it. My brother and I thought it was pretty funny, and that's when Dad said he would give a dollar to the one who could keep his goddamn mouth shut the longest. We would always have a couple flat tires on the trip but Dad would just keep driving and swearing until he found a gas station.

One year my brother won a yo-yo contest and the prize was an all paid vacation to Fort Lauderdale for the whole family. It was a very long week. Mom was so sunburned she ended up in bed. Dad had bought a swim suit and matching shirt and the first time we went to the beach he got slapped by a huge wave and knocked flat in the sand. After a string of cuss words he stormed back to the room got dressed and spent the rest of the trip in the bar. On the way home we stopped in St. Augustine, to visit the wax museum. My brother ran into a glass door and nearly did himself in. He didn't break the glass, but had a huge black eye. Of course, I thought it was extremely funny and got in trouble for laughing. On a trip to the Ozarks, Dad almost killed us all when he hit the dock at about 30 miles per hour. It was my fault because I had to go the bathroom. The committee in my head began telling me when things went wrong it was usually my fault.

The only fun trip we had was to Wisconsin Dells. No major problems however we got some strange looks from other drivers. We brought our parakeet "Ike" with us and we let him lose in the car. Ike liked to hang upside down, and dangle from your hair to look in your eyes. He also liked to sit on the steering wheel and look outside. He would bop up and down to music, shaking his wings and screeching. It was quite a site to see and a little distracting to other drivers.

# 4

## *Here Come The Resentments*

Kath and I were planning on going to St. Scholastica High School after eight grade, and then the unbelievable happened: Dad announced he was starting his own business and we were moving to St. Louis. I felt my world had just crashed around me. I pleaded with Mom and Dad not to move, but they told me to stop whining and I would make new friends.

We moved to Ballwin, MO. about twenty-five miles from downtown St. Louis. Dad had found a house, which was exciting, as we had always lived in apartments. The house was out in the boonies and there was a cow in our front yard one day. I was used to city noises and places to go, things to do, and there was nothing in Ballwin. I met a girl who lived further down the street but she was only interested in stalking boys, and we had very little in common. I felt alone, afraid, hurt, and angry. The committee now had a list of resentments to discuss.

My Mom insisted I join the CYC (Catholic Youth Council) at Church, and she put my name on the ballot for the May Queen election. Well, I won, to my mother's delight, and I was just mortified when I found out that Mom and Dad had donated the altar cross at the new church in memory of my Grandfather. I knew that was the reason I was elected May Queen. The May King's mother sewed altar covers and vestments and that is why he won. We were supposed to represent the church in a parade and a dance, and neither one of us wanted to be there. A match made by controlling parents. Another resentment added to the list.

I was supposed to go to Coyle High School, a Catholic coed school, but after we moved, we found out that Coyle had closed, and I had to enroll in a different school. Mom decided to enroll me in an all girls' high school, St. Joseph's Academy. I liked the school, but making friends was hard.

Everyone had gone to grade school together and I felt like an outsider. There were two girls that I had gone to first and second grade with, but they were not interested in bringing me into their clique. I was on my own the first year, and I was just miserable. The summer after my freshman year, Kath came to visit and went with us to Colorado. It was the most fun I had since moving and I was so upset when she left. I wanted to go back to Skokie and my friends.

After sophomore year started a new girl, named Jan, arrived from Connecticut, and she was as miserable about moving as I was. We started to talk and became friends. We didn't socialize outside of school since I lived so far away, but it made the days at school tolerable. In my sophomore year, we moved into the subdivision where Jan lived. I met other girls who went to St. Joe's and we could all walk to each other's homes. I began to make friends in and outside of school. I really loved St. Joe's. I made good grades and played field hockey, volleyball and basketball. The recreation room at school had a record player, and some of us brought in 45's and started dancing. Before long, the rec room was the place to be, and everybody was dancing. I was back in my comfort zone—dancing.

The nuns who taught at St. Joe's were young and we had a great time with them. Only Sister Dolores was a crab. She taught Latin and kept index cards for each student. If you saw her writing on your card, you knew she was pissed. Sister Theresa was our favorite. She could not have been but four or five years older than we were. I taught Sister Theresa how to drive a stick shift, and I can still see her veil flying in the wind as she drove my Falcon convertible around the school parking lot. Sister William taught Biology and although she caught us smoking in the bathroom, she pretended not to notice and did not tell Mother Superior. We tee-peed the convent one night, and snuck into the home economics room and spent the night. We found out much later that the nuns knew we had stayed the night, but we never got in trouble. It was all harmless fun and we never did anything destructive. Apparently, our reputation of having fun followed us for some time after graduation, as one of Trey's girlfriends, who went to school at St. Joe's, said she had heard about the class of 1963 from one of the nuns.

Dad had started his railroad supply business when we moved to St. Louis. As most alcoholics know, we hate people telling us what to do, and Dad was fed up with his job at Standard Oil. His business was proving to be very successful, and in my junior year, Mom and Dad built a home in an adjacent subdivision. It was a beautiful home and I was still close to all my friends.

Mom and Dad seemed to change when they became financially well off. They never had money and I remember them talking about living over a greenhouse when they were first married, and that my first bed was a dresser drawer. They had met in Grand Junction, CO. when Mom was the ticket girl and Dad was an usher at the local theater. Mom was eighteen, Dad was seventeen when they married, and they had to get permission from Dad's mom to marry. They really struggled the years Dad was in the Navy. Mom worked at a candy factory when Dad was overseas, and I remember her telling me how angry she was at having to pay rent to live with Dad's mom when she was trying to save enough to move out. She had that resentment for sixty-three years. My family was always big on resentments—rehearsing for retaliation we call it today.

When the money started coming in Dad became the big spender. He always had a new car, sent friends on expensive trips, bought friends expensive gifts, showered Mom with beautiful jewelry, and joined a country club. He went to the bar every day, came home and raised hell, and went to bed around 4:00PM every day. He would get up at 4:00AM, all bright and cheery with no memory of what he did the night before, and how he had hurt Mom with his mean accusations and filthy mouth. On weekends, there was always a barbecue at our house and Dad would manage to insult someone and ruin the day.

Mom took up golf and gardening, but her passion was to make sure we looked good. Don't think, don't feel, and don't cry. No matter how bad something may be, suck it up and pretend all is well.. Even after years of emotional and physical abuse from Dad, she would continue to enable him, make excuses for his behavior, and was very defensive of him and his actions. If Ralph or I would attempt to defend her while Dad was verbally attacking her, she would beg us to just let it go, as defending her made it worse. So we all played the game and never mentioned the elephant in the living room. We sat and watched King Alcohol tear apart our family and we did nothing.

When I turned sixteen, Dad took me to a Ford Dealer to pick out a car. He told me to choose among three cars: a 1957 turquoise Thunderbird, a navy blue Ford Falcon convertible, and a red something or other, I don't remember. I picked the Thunderbird. It had white leather interior and it was my dream car. Dad said that was not the right choice, and I should have picked the Falcon. The committee reminded me that one more time I screwed up. I drove the Falcon home. Since it was up to me to keep the car running, I got my first job as a locker attendant at a country club down the street. Another girl I knew, Mary, worked there also, and she had the keys to lock up in the evening. She also had the key to the club itself, and after work we would go to the clubhouse and drink 3.2 Falstaff draft beer. Awful stuff, but I loved the way it made me feel. I worked at the pool two summers and had the usual crush on the lifeguard. I managed to make a real pest out of myself when he was around. He was a few years older and never gave me the time of day. Mary and I played strip poker one night with the two lifeguards and got royally drunk on beer. It sure released the inhibitions. I would come home at night and stagger to my room. I was caught one night when I tripped over the ottoman and almost went through the window. I thought it was funny, Mom didn't. She also caught me one night in the kitchen drinking a vodka and orange juice. She slapped the drink out of my hand and then smacked me, saying, "You're going to be just like your father." What I was beginning to figure out, was *why* Dad drank. With each swallow of alcohol, all my insecurities disappeared.

Alcohol began to sneak into my life. My friends and I would go out every Friday and Saturday night, and there was always drinking. We would hang around outside a liquor store and pay some guy to buy us a case of beer. We spent weekends driving back and forth between hamburger stands, scoping out the guys. One Saturday night, my friend, Casey, got in a friend's Corvette and started down a busy street drag racing. She drifted over the center line and hit another car head-on at eighty miles an hour. She was killed instantly. It should have been a wake-up call for all of us, but it was not. I was not able to go to her funeral as we were leaving for Colorado that day. I begged my parents to let me stay with Jan so I could go to the funeral, but they said no. Since money was not a problem, I asked to stay and fly in later that evening, and they said no. I was so angry and I hung on to that resentment for many years. They just didn't understand that I had to be there to say goodbye.

We had heard about a band that played at the Sunset Country Club and we decided to go hear the band play. There was an abundance of alcohol, the band was incredible, and the room filled with the best dancers I had ever seen. I watched and learned how to dance the "Imperial" and I felt I had died and gone to heaven. Every Saturday night was spent at the Sunset Club. The band was called "The Ike and Tina Turner Review," and they were wild, and played sensational music. Hard to believe that Tina Turner was only a couple years older than me at the time. My parents had forbidden me to go there, but I went anyway. I had to go. I lived to drink and dance. The combination of alcohol and dancing was the magic potion. It made me feel the way everybody else felt without drinking. This was in 1963, the year of the "Kingsmen" and the song "Louie, Louie." If you saw the movie *Dirty Dancing*, this was exactly how we danced back then, and at some dance clubs, we were told to "clean it up" or we would be asked to leave.

The last two years of high school we were all dating and some of us were "going steady." We went to parties, danced, and drank. We would be so drunk that I know God had to be watching over us. I am so grateful we never got hurt or injured someone. One of the boy's dads owned a boat rental in the Ozarks and we would go to the lake on weekends and cook dinner for them. In return, we could have a boat and water ski at no charge. We did this several times a summer and it was always a fun time. Joe was a professional skier, and taught a class in water skiing at the lake. Joe died of injuries he sustained in Vietnam.

I dated several guys in high school, and if they could not dance, they didn't last long with me. One guy I loved to dance with was Jack. He was such a good dancer and we had a lot of fun. We were just friends and only went out to dance, but my parents forbade me to see him because he was Korean. His Dad, while in the Korean War, adopted Jack. He was polite and a good student, just a real nice guy. Every time I hear the song "Theme from A Summer Place," I think of Jack. He would be the first of a long list of boys my parents didn't like and would forbid me to date. In my senior year I dated several boys who were all frowned on by my parents. I was never given a reason, just a disgusting shake of the head with "Can't you do better than that?" Sometimes Mom would actually laugh when my date showed up, and I remember the time she said, "I hope you don't see anybody we know." The committee: "Dana, can't you do anything right?" "Can't you even find a decent boyfriend?" "What's the matter with you?"

# 5

## *Let the Party Begin*

When it was time to look at colleges, Dad and I drove to the University of Oklahoma and the University of Kansas to look at the campus. I wanted to go to the School of Journalism at the University of Colorado in Boulder, but Mom and Dad nixed that idea because it was too far away. My grandmother still lived in Denver, my other grandmother in Colorado Springs, and my Uncle Bullus lived in Littleton. It is not like there wasn't any family around. Since I had my heart set on going to Boulder, I really wasn't interested in the other universities and I decided to stay at home and go to St. Louis University. There was also a part of me that was afraid of what Dad would do to Mom if I were gone. His drinking was out of control and he was a mean drunk. I know Mom wanted me to stay at home, and I guess I felt guilty going away and leaving her to deal with Dad. Guilt—the gift that keeps on giving.

I remember the day I went to register for the first semester as a freshman. I was in the gym and was so overwhelmed with everything I wanted to run. I was scared to death as, one more time, everyone but me seemed to know what to do and where to go. The campus seemed huge to me and I knew no one. I was too slow in picking classes and every time I thought I had my schedule done a class would be full and I would have to start over. I know I was in that gym a good five hours and I had not even gotten my books yet. Used books could be purchased, but of course, they were already gone and I had to buy new ones. I could not believe how much these textbooks cost. The first week of school I was late for every class and so frustrated I could scream. I did find the café in the basement of Chouteau House, and I would go there between classes. It was there that I finally met some other freshmen that were just as frazzled as me, and some who had the same classes I did and at the same time. I eventually figured out where I was supposed to be and at what time, and started to settle into a routine. My classes started at eight every morning, and since I was living at home, I would get up at six, be on the highway by seven in order to find a parking place, and be on time for class. Today, I still have dreams about being late for class, not being able to find a parking space, forgetting my books, and being lost on campus.

At freshmen get-togethers there were always upper classmen hanging around checking out the newbies, and I started meeting guys. However, I was so scared, insecure, and lacking in social skills that I would dread these encounters. There were a couple of dances for the freshmen, and if I could have a few drinks before the dances, I had fun. It didn't take me long to hook up with the drinking fraternity. They danced, they drank, and I had found my place. I came in second (missed by one vote) at the freshmen queen election, but was chosen to ride on the drinking fraternity's float on parade day. Alcohol did for me what I could not do for myself. I partied on weekends, but not during the week, as I had to study to keep decent grades. In my sophomore year, I changed majors, physical therapy to sociology. After two tries, I just could not get more than a "D" in statistics, and I absolutely hated Chemistry. I had four-hour labs twice a week and I didn't have a clue what was going on. I would have to hitchhike to the medical school and I was always late. I didn't like to drive to class, as it was impossible to find a parking place. In fact, the first ticket I ever got was for speeding to get to this class. The committee was very active again, the mantra being "You are so dumb that you have to change majors." Mom and Dad are going to be so disappointed." "One more time you messed up."

In the fall of 1964 a most wonderful thing happened—Beatlemania. The first song I heard was "I Wanna Hold Your Hand," and it is still my favorite Beatles song. The campus went nuts, and you could hear Beatle music everywhere. On highway 40, on the way to school, you could hear the sounds of the Beatles from car radios. Every party we went to played nothing but the Beatles. I still remember seeing them on the Ed Sullivan show and I saw them when they came to St. Louis. It was an incredible experience. What a thrill to see the Beatles.

In my junior year, I dated a couple guys from the dental school, and a couple of law school students. I was in no hurry to get serious with anyone, although there was one law student who I was dating that I really liked. However, one more time, Mom and Dad found something wrong with him, and I could not subject him to any more embarrassing confrontations with my parents. There was one boy Joe, who I was forbidden to date because of his last name. Mom and Dad insisted he was Jewish and I told them he was not Jewish, he was German. I even had one of Mom's friends call her and verify he was German. It didn't make any difference since his name still sounded Jewish! My punishment for going out with someone they didn't like was a veil of silence. Sometimes the silence would go on for a week. I dated one guy in spite of their objections, and they were so rude to him and hateful to me that I stopped seeing him. It was just a no-win situation.

A friend of mine was dating a guy on the baseball team, and she fixed me up with Tom who played on the team. Chris and I would go to the local games and go to the out-of-town games to cheer the team on. Tom was a very nice guy, but lived and breathed baseball. Nothing serious ever developed, but we were both OK with that. We became very good friends, and I even introduced Tom to the girl he married. My parents never met Tom, never even knew about him. I was not going to let them belittle one of the nicest guys I had ever met.

I did manage to bring home a few guys that Mom and Dad didn't ridicule. The problem was I didn't like them enough to date them more than two or three times. My parents would be very upset if I stopped seeing someone they liked, and the silent treatment would follow. These guys were the ones who didn't drink, and had no interest in dancing and parties. They were good, respectable, and motivated guys, who had promising careers ahead of them. I thought they were boring and didn't know how to have a good time. Alcohol had its hold on me, and dictated who I spent time with and what I did. Alcohol was taking me to places I didn't want to go; I just didn't know it at the time. The more I drank the less the committee bothered me.

When I was a junior, I went to a law school fraternity barbecue. I still remember sitting on the grass talking with a friend when something caught my attention. I looked up and saw this guy coming around the corner of the house and all I could do was stare. He was one of the pledges and I knew in an instant that he was the one I would marry. He was about 5'9", nice build, brown hair, and a terrific smile. When he walked over and said "Hi" I just melted. His name was Fran, and we immediately connected. He asked if I would like to go to a friend's party in Gaslight Square. In the mid-sixties, Gaslight Square was the center of entertainment in St. Louis. There were restaurants, clubs, and bars, and many celebrities got their start at the Square. I remember seeing Bobby Darin, Woody Allen, Phyllis Diller and the Smother Brothers. Fran's friend had an apartment over a bar and we danced, drank, and had a great time. The police had curfew raids back then, and the police came knocking at the door and sent us all home. Fran took me home and said he would call. I remember telling Mom the next day that I had found the guy I was going to marry. I told her he was Irish Catholic and a freshman in SLU Law School. His Dad was an attorney, and he had one brother, a sister, and twin sisters, his Mom didn't work and they lived in Bellfontaine Neighbors in North County. It seemed to me that he certainly had all the qualifications to meet my parent's approval, but true to form, the first comments were: "Francis?" "Who would want to live that far north?" The committee said, "One more time you made a poor choice." I refused to listen to the committee. This time I was determined to do it my way. I turned off my ears to any negatives that were said, and Fran and I started seeing each other.

During the week, Fran and I would meet before class for a cup of coffee. If we had a couple hours between classes, we would go to Usselmann's Deli for a cornbeef sandwich and a six pack of beer. We would then go to Forest Park, have lunch and just walk around the park. After school, we would meet in the parking lot and drink a six-pack, then go to the Sixty-One Club on Lindell for a couple beers. They never asked for ID's at the club and we would meet our friends there on the weekends. Since I had all the classes needed to graduate, I spent my senior year studying to pass the orals at the end of the year. Fran had a hellish schedule in law school, and dropped out in the second year. He said he was only there to please his Dad, and had no interest in continuing. Fran's dad blamed me for his not finishing law school. My committee blamed me too, but it was no big deal after a few drinks.

We went out to dinner on the weekends, took in a movie, or went to a party, and usually ended the evening at The Mainlander Bar drinking Impatient Virgins and Suffering Bastards. (They were rum based and really hit you hard.) Or, we would go to the Fox and Hounds Bar and drink a champagne and red wine mixture from yard beer glasses. We spent a lot of time with a couple that also liked to drink and party, and we would bar hop from The Puppet Pub to The Hobby Horse in Clayton. We also went to a Jazz club downtown where The Ramsey Lewis Trio played. We spent time on the river at a friend's cabin, and went to Meramec State Park several times a year. Everything we did revolved around drinking, and both Fran and I were drinking to excess. We were well past social drinking and into problem drinking. I have always liked the definition of a social drinker, "If you have a drink, so shall I."

Fran's temper would surface after drinking too much, and I saw him grab a baseball bat and go after some guy at a picnic. I do not know what provoked him, but we had to literally tackle Fran to stop him from hitting the guy. At the weekend barbecues at my house, the mingling of beer, scotch, and gin, always resulted in an argument between Fran and Dad. They were both very opinionated, and the verbal sparring was constant. Thank God, it was always a verbal war and no punches were ever thrown. Now in Fran's family there was always a verbal attack of some kind and fists flying. Fran and his brother John detested each other, and you could not even leave them alone in a room. John was always fighting with his Dad, and one of the twin girls was always antagonizing Fran. John left home at sixteen, and the family heard from him maybe three times a year. In retrospect, he was probably the smartest one of the bunch getting away from the craziness at home. While we were dating, Fran never raised a hand to me. We would have verbal spats, but nothing serious, and always when we were drinking.

Fran and I were engaged in September of 1967. It was a total surprise to me when he gave me the ring. I eagerly accepted, and it seemed that Fran and Dad had called a truce. I was surprised when Fran asked Dad for permission to marry me and Dad said "Yes." We wanted to be married in February, just a small wedding and small reception. Neither one of us wanted a big bash. Well, that didn't go over at all. My Mom had a fit and informed us we were having a big wedding and a big reception. It was part of that "looking good" syndrome my Mom had. She also nixed the February date and insisted on May 1968.

Shortly after Fran and I were engaged, his parents invited my family for dinner at Scott Air Force Base in Belleville, IL. It was a very long night. Our two families had absolutely nothing in common and conversation was strained. Mom and Dad were already pissed that they had to drive to Belleville to eat dinner, and since Dad was asked to take it easy on the gin and Squirt, he was antsy and irritable. We were all glad when it was time to go, and from then on, Mom and Dad seldom saw or spoke to Fran's family.

Always looking good was so important to Mom. She told me how to get my hair styled, and would drag me to these fancy stores in Clayton to buy clothes. She insisted I wear Pendleton slacks and blazers, and everything had to match. I hated what she wanted me to wear but it was not worth the silent treatment to argue with her. She didn't understand how stupid I looked on campus with my perfect little outfits with matching shoes and purses. I felt like a clown. I started putting clothes in my car so I could change after I got to school.

When I started looking for a job after graduation, my Dad dragged me downtown to meet a local newscaster. The station was looking for a substitute weather girl and Dad thought I would be perfect. Oh my God! I had to audition and I was absolutely awful and scared to death. Dad was not pleased with me, saying I had blown this opportunity to have a great job. I didn't look good, so none of us looked good. Dad and Mom were both so angry with me. They refused to listen to me when I told them I didn't want to be a weather girl, and they kept repeating, "How could you do that to us?" "How could you be so selfish?" The committee was in full session too: "You should feel guilty about letting your parents down." "Dad pulled a lot of strings to get you that interview and you should be ashamed of yourself." "No matter what you do it's always wrong." "They have done so much for you couldn't you have tried a little harder to get the job?"

And on, and on, ad infinitum. I just felt like screaming," Would someone please listen to me?" "Does anyone care about what I want?" One more time I survived the silent treatment, knowing that it wouldn't be the last.

# 6

## *My Big Fat Catholic Wedding*

Making plans for the wedding was a nightmare. Everything had to be done Mom's way or not at all. I had no input regarding the arrangements and anything I said was discounted. I didn't want this huge wedding, especially since Fran and I didn't even know most of the people being invited, but Mom insisted that all of Dad's business friends needed to be invited. Our Church was just not fancy enough to be married in, so Mom arranged for us to be married at the Old Cathedral downtown, and Dad knew a Monsignor who agreed to perform the ceremony. It was all unbelievable, and I finally threw in the towel, there was no need for my input. The reception was at Trader Vic's downtown, and it would be a buffet. I must have tried on fifty dresses until Mom found the one she liked at the most expensive store in St. Louis. The bridesmaid dresses were to be the same color as the carpeting at the Cathedral, the cake made by the most expensive bakery in St. Louis, and my clothes for the honeymoon from Talbots a fancy store in Clayton. The invitations were black print on a cream color, and five hundred were ordered in case we had to add somebody to the list. Formal pictures of me in my wedding dress were taken and sent to the papers. I felt like crawling in a hole. The committee: "Your opinion doesn't matter." "Mom can't trust you to pick out the wedding dress." "If you choose something your Mom doesn't like it will ruin the wedding." "You have no idea what you are doing." "You make poor decisions, that's why Mom is doing everything."

The rehearsal dinner was at Fran's house. Of course, Mom and Dad thought it should be at a fancy restaurant because it looked good, but the dinner turned out very nice. It was catered, and had an open bar which made Dad happy. My brother had champagne for the first time and he was deathly sick the next morning. In fact, he says he hasn't touched champagne since.

The wedding was at 10:00AM on Saturday, May 4, 1968. It was a beautiful day. I remember waking up and thinking, "Thank God it's almost over." We had five limos to take everyone to church. We gathered in the back of church and waited for everyone to be seated. We were forty-five minutes early, so we all just stood around watching people. Mom always had this thing about being early, and it could be very annoying at times. When it was finally 10:00AM, Dad walked me down the aisle, and as I looked at the faces of the guests, I had no idea who half these people were. It was a long ceremony, almost two hours, and then we received a Papal Blessing certificate from Rome (enough already Mom). We then had pictures taken, and that went on forever with Mom telling the photographer what to do, and who should be included in the pictures. Then off to Trader Vic's for the reception. It took hours to get everyone through the reception line and the reception party alone went through twelve cases of champagne. Then off to the buffet, where there was an enormous amount of food. I didn't have an appetite, but I managed to get a few scotch and waters down to stop the anxiety. Mom and Dad were constantly introducing me to people whom I would never see again; and Mom whispering to me "Stand up straight!" I never really had a chance to enjoy the reception. Fran and I then changed clothes and went back to the reception so everyone could throw rice and say goodbye. The wedding party came with us to the airport, where we sat in the bar and made fools out of ourselves. An argument ensued with another wedding party at the airport who had the same bridesmaid dresses only in a different color. Someone said the pink was prettier than the green and since the other party was also drunk, it got kind of ugly. As we boarded the plane to fly to Jamaica, a limo was waiting to take the wedding party back to Mom and Dads for the party after the party.

We had a flight to Miami with a stop in Atlanta. All the drinks at the Atlanta airport were doubles, and we managed to down a few and talk about how glad we were that it was over. Fran was a good sport through all the planning, and he knew that we just had to let Mom do her thing, but the honeymoon was what we planned and we were excited about the trip. We arrived in Jamaica the following morning and rented a car. Learning how to drive on the wrong side of the road is not easy. You have to drive fast or the other drivers will run you over. They honk and yell and I was a nervous wreck by the time we got to the Bermuda Inn. Jamaica is a beautiful island, and the Inn was on a secluded part of the beach. The water was so clear, and a turquoise blue, and the island smells like jasmine all the time. Waiters would bring drinks to us on the beach, we had dinner every evening on the patio, and the food was so good. There were musicians every evening and it was a very romantic place. We went to the Playboy Club one evening, met a couple and spent a day sightseeing with them. We drove through the mountains one day on the way to Kingston, and the scenery was breathtaking. There were waterfalls every where and bright patches of color on the hills. We went deep sea fishing one day, and I had a great time, while Fran, the captain, and the crew spent half the trip puking over the side of the boat. We both caught a couple of dolphins (not the Flipper kind), and the cook prepared them for dinner. I hate fish, and Fran was still green from the trip, so the crew ate the fish. Seven days later we flew home and we were broke and had to borrow money to call for a ride home.

# 7

## *Away From Home*

I had started work at the St. Louis City Juvenile Court the year before we married. I was a domestic court officer and made determinations on which parent should have the children in contested custody cases. I loved my job, and was good at it. I visited homes in bad neighborhoods but always felt safe since people thought I was the welfare check lady. I remember going into Pruitt-Igoe projects, alone. We didn't carry anything but mace and I never needed to use it during the two years I worked there. Occasionally, I would go to court if the judge wanted to talk to me, but most of the time I just submitted my report to the court. The last few months I worked there, I started lying about having a home visit in the late afternoon and would meet friends at a bar. That is when I developed a taste for martinis with pickled brussel sprouts. This almost became a daily routine, since Fran was traveling with his new job. We had a nice apartment, and most of the tenants were single or newly married, and invited me over when Fran was gone. We drank every evening, and got up and went to work the next day just to do it all over again.

Fran had first gone to work for an insurance company, but soon found a job as a sales rep for a railroad. The following spring Fran had to relocate to Louisville, KY. for six months. He didn't pressure me to go, as he knew I liked my job, but after two incidents at work, I decided to put in my two weeks. The first happened in my office. I had a very angry client come in waving a knife and screaming at me. I hit the buzzer under my desk and Officer Gant smashed through the door, grabbed this guy and literally picked him up off the floor and threw him into the hallway. The second happened when I was walking down Lindell Blvd. after having lunch at a Chinese restaurant on the corner. I was heading for my car when I heard running behind me. I turned around and there were three teenagers coming at me. I slipped off my shoes and ran like hell to my car. I was able to get in and lock the doors before they reached me. I laid on the horn, they took off, and I thought, "I'm not sure I want to do this anymore."

We kept our apartment in St. Louis since we would only be in Louisville six months. Fran found a studio apartment at a downtown hotel. It was a combination bedroom and living room, bathroom, and tiny kitchen. Every day I would walk to the IGA, get something to cook for dinner, grab a sandwich for lunch from a little café, and watch soap operas until Fran came home. I didn't have a car and the neighborhood was not the best, so I just hung around the hotel all day. I soon began making the daily trip to the liquor store around the corner. I was drinking a half bottle of Ushers scotch every day, and pouring some back in the bottle from my spare so Fran wouldn't know how much I was drinking. He knew I was miserable and suggested I go back home. I took the train home and it was such a relief to be back at our apartment. It was only a geographic, as I continued to drink every day. Actually, I drank more since Fran was not around to tell me I was drinking too much.

When Fran came home from Louisville, he told me the company was transferring us to Corpus Christi, TX. I knew we would be moving as Fran's position as a sales rep required relocating, and I was excited about this move. The railroad packed everything for us, including putting my Falcon on a flat car, and we drove to Texas. My Mom was so sad when we left, and the committee reminded me: "Don't you feel guilty about leaving her?" "She's going to be miserable the whole time you are gone," "What's she going to do without you running interference between her and Dad?" "This move is breaking her heart." Again, alcohol numbed the noise in my head,

We found an apartment on the fourth floor of a high rise across the street from the bay. It is a beautiful city, and I loved Corpus Christi. When boredom began to settle in, I did what I usually did: I drank. I decided to do volunteer work at Spohn Hospital, but didn't stay long, as I preferred staying home and drinking. I joined a ladies golf group and played twice a week but didn't sign up to play again. Fran was gone a lot and I would pack a cooler of beer and go to Padre Island a couple times a week. Back then (1969-1970) the only things on Padre Island was a snack shack and an occasional dock for fishing. No condominiums, no college kids. It was a beautiful place and only a half-hour drive from home. I would drive home drunk and I know God was watching out for me, and thankfully, the others on the road.

I would occasionally see the lady who lived down the hall. She seemed nice and one day invited me in for a drink. I was lonely for someone to talk to and we began spending a lot of time together. It didn't take me long to realize that she was an alcoholic. She sat and drank all evening and I began to join her when Fran was gone. In fact, when Fran was in town, I could not wait for him to leave again so I could go next door and drink. Bobbie was drinking over a past marriage, and a husband who walked out on her. She would cry and carry on about how she still loved him, and wished she could see him again. Since Bobbie was providing the scotch, I gladly listened.

In August of 1969, we moved to Houston, TX. However, the week we were to move, hurricane Celia came roaring into Corpus. We had very little warning as the storm was heading to the Louisiana coast but turned west at the last minute. It was a terrifying experience. We were on the fourth floor of our apartment building huddled against the walls with other residents. To feel a concrete reinforced building sway is frightening, and the roar of the wind unforgettable. We could hear glass breaking, furniture being thrown around the apartments, children crying, adults praying. I will never forget looking out one of the windows and seeing the wind blowing the water right out of the bay. The following morning it was utter devastation. All the windows were blown out and I could see furniture floating in the bay, with pieces of boats and unrecognizable debris. The elevator was sucked right out of the building and was in the parking lot. We lost everything stored in our locker in the basement, and what was left in the apartment was covered with mold and mildew. My only concern was whether the liquor stores were open. We had drunk all the beer and scotch and I was beginning to panic. Bobbie was also becoming very anxious, and she went out and bought all the scotch she could find. King

Alcohol was running my life; I could not function without it. After a week, we finally had electricity, and water, and we moved to Houston two weeks later.

# 8

## *Why Is This Happening?*

We found a small apartment in Houston and Fran began travelling almost every week. I was lonely and picked up the bottle. I never met anyone in the complex and stayed at home reading novels and drinking alone. I desperately wanted a baby (I think what I wanted was unconditional love), and in December 1970, I found out I was pregnant. We were thrilled. I cut back on my drinking, but never considered stopping. Of course, back then no one had ever heard of fetal alcohol syndrome.

I had a very easy pregnancy and Trey was born on July 14, 1971. Fran didn't come in the labor room or the delivery room, which was fine with me, as he almost passed out when we took the pre-wedding blood tests. I thought I had an idea what to expect (don't believe what you read in the books), but I was wrong and absolutely terrified. I remember the pain was indescribable, as the anesthesiologist waited too long to give me the saddle block. I was awake when Trey was born and it was instant love. Back then new mothers stayed in the hospital for seven days, and could only see their baby for feedings. Mom, Dad, and my brother came to visit and although I was glad to see them, my Mom immediately started in, "How can you stand it here, the apartment is so small?" "This is the hottest place I have ever been." "Why do you have a fireplace? You would never use it living here." When Trey was two months old, we went back home to St. Louis. We found an apartment in the same complex we lived after we were married. I was a stay-at-home Mom, a perfect setup for a blooming alcoholic.

When the telephone rang that morning before Trey's baptism, and Mom told me Bullus had died, I was so angry with God. I was to remain angry with God for years. I just could not understand why He had to take her before she saw Trey. Not that I needed her death as an excuse to drink

(I could always find an excuse of some kind), I again started drinking every day. I was in real trouble with alcohol and would leave Trey alone to drive to the liquor store to stock up on scotch. I began store hopping so no one would notice how often I bought booze. Fran never said anything about my drinking, I guess because I was a functional drunk. There was always food on the table, the house was clean, and Trey was happy and healthy.

We moved to another apartment when Trey was two. It was a nicer place and more centrally located. Everything I needed was within walking distance. It was the summer of 1973, I was trying controlled drinking, (instead of eight or nine, I would have five or six), and we had a new baby on the way. Fran was still working as a sales rep for the railroad and he seemed to enjoy his job. We didn't have any money problems, so I could not figure out what was bothering him. He suddenly became very quiet. He would sit and stare out the window, and had difficulty carrying on a conversation. He had no interest in Trey, or me, and when I asked him what was wrong he would just stare at me. I chose to ignore what was going on hoping it would just disappear. (Alcoholics are very good at doing that.) Fran continued to work but eventually he was asked by the company to see their counselor. He had a few sessions and was referred to a psychiatrist. He never told me what was discussed, but he took a leave of absence from work. He sat, stared, said people were following him and talking about him, and he was suspicious of everyone. If a helicopter flew over he was convinced they were looking for him. When the football players were in the huddle, he insisted they were talking about him. Bright lights terrified him. I felt sorry for him, but was also mad as hell at him. I absolutely didn't know what to do as my world came tumbling down around me. It got worse as we went into the Christmas season with all the blinking lights. He would stare at the lights and was almost catatonic at times. It was obvious Fran had a mental problem, and I had tried numerous times to talk to the psychiatrist. I left messages, and he returned my call one time. He said that I had to be patient, and it may take weeks for the drugs to work. I didn't think I had weeks. I was seven months pregnant and so angry and frustrated.

We went to Mom and Dad's for Christmas dinner on December 23, 1973. Fran was acting very strange and thought every comment made was about him. In the middle of dinner, he left the table saying he needed to get something out of the car. When he didn't return in several minutes I went outside and the car was gone. Trey and I stayed at Mom and Dad's that night and at 2:00 the following morning a police officer in East St. Louis called to say they had Fran. He was found wandering the streets and incoherent. Dad and my brother went to East St. Louis to get him and the car, and brought Fran back to the house. He had nothing to say and just stared. We went home and cleaned up as we were due at his parents for Christmas Eve dinner. Have you ever noticed that when life goes bad it's always a weekend or holiday?

Fran's family was aware that something was wrong, but blamed it on stress. They would not accept that he was mentally ill and needed help, and were sure that after the holidays he would be fine. As we sat down to eat dinner, Fran left the table and went out the front door. To prevent a repeat of last night I went out after him. He was going to the car and I yelled for him to stop. He turned, and started to run towards me. He stopped, took off his shoes and threw them at me, and came at me with such a look of hate I screamed. His Dad came outside and physically stopped Fran before he could hurt me. As his Dad talked to him I went inside and called the doctor he was seeing. I was told to take him to St. Mary's ER. His Dad drove and the silence was deafening. We had two options, involuntary commitment, or seeing the doctor as an outpatient after the holidays. Mr. Nolan said, "No, I will not force him to go in the hospital." I said, "Yes, I will sign the commitment papers." Fran's Dad was not happy with my decision, but I could not continue living under the present circumstances. Fran was in the hospital December 24, 1973 until February 12, 1974. The diagnosis was paranoid schizophrenia. I would get up in the morning, take Trey to Mom and Dad's, and spend the day in the hospital. I would leave around 6:00 p.m., pick up Trey and go home. Fran was in a locked ward and I hated having to go in there. The first couple weeks, Fran was quiet and suspicious of me, and seldom talked except to ask why he was in the hospital. He didn't seem to care if I was there or not.

The patients on the ward were frightening to be around. One guy ripped the fire extinguisher off the wall and started spraying everyone; there were fights over what to watch on TV, or where someone was supposed to sit. Some of the days were endless and I felt my world tumbling. I felt I had abandoned Trey, and I was so worried about the effects of all this stress on my pregnancy. After Fran had been in the hospital about three weeks, he seemed better and happy to see me. He was allowed to go with me outside the ward and walk in the hall. One time he tried to bolt through the outside door but I was able to grab him and calm him down. That ended our walks.

After Fran was released from the hospital, he seemed better, but he was not the man I married. The Fran I knew was gone, and I would never see him again.

During this time, I would have a couple drinks in the evening after picking Trey up, but I was so tired, both emotionally and physically, that I didn't have the energy to drink. Fran was released from the hospital on February 12, 1974, and Mark was born on February 22. Mark seemed just fine when he was born, but a couple hours later a priest came in to tell me they were taking Mark to Cardinal Glennon Hospital. The neonatal nurse said Mark was having difficulty breathing and he needed to be transferred immediately. They wheeled me out in the hall so I could see Mark, and as they were leaving, I asked the priest to baptize him. Mark was in an incubator and surrounded by nurses and doctors who would accompany him to the hospital.

# 9

## *Go Away, God*

My doctor let me leave the hospital a couple days early so I could go to Cardinal Glennon to be with Mark. However, the first place I went was not the hospital, but a bar on an adjacent street. My committee was working overtime, and I had to stop the meeting in my head. My brain was racing: "Why was this happening?" "What did I do, or not do, to deserve this?" "Is Fran ever going to be well?" "If not, what am I going to do?" "I want to run, I can't live like this." "No matter what I do it always turns out wrong." "Have you noticed the 'I told you so' looks on Mom and Dad's face?" *Please, shut up, shut up*! As I sat in that bar drinking the committee away, I looked up and told God: "No more! No more church, no more prayers, no more you! Get out of my life! I don't understand why you are doing this to me, and I can't take anymore!"

My Mom and I took turns at the hospital with Mark so one of us could be with Trey. Everyday we would rock him and feed him, and sometimes it would take an hour to get an ounce of formula down him. Fran would be there also, and I kept watch in case he ran. The doctors could not find what was wrong with Mark. They did many tests, including barium x-rays, blood tests, urine tests etc. and eventually decided it was a congenital heart abnormality. We took Mark home after twelve days in the hospital. He was on a heart monitor and I don't think I slept at all the first month for fear of not hearing the monitor go off. Fran was still in a zombie state, and between watching him, taking care of Trey, and being on guard with Mark, I was exhausted. My Dad would take Fran to the hospital for weekly shock treatments, and I would take Mark to the doctor every week. As much as my Dad detested Fran and angry that I married him, he was willing to help us during this time.

Fran went back to work and he seemed to be doing better. The doctors took Mark off the heart monitor and he was doing fine; and Trey was so excited to have a baby brother. In March, we transferred to Kansas City. Fran went ahead of us to find an apartment, as the doctors didn't want to release Mark from their care for another couple of months. In May 1974, we packed up the boys and went to Kansas City. We had a referral to see a pediatric cardiologist and after several visits he released Mark from his care, saying he could find nothing wrong, and the heart murmur had disappeared. That was wonderful news. We really liked our place in Kansas City. It was large enough, two bedrooms, two baths, and I was very happy there. Trey had kids to play with, and I made friends with several women. My drinking didn't seem to be a problem as far as I was concerned. I drank every day, but didn't get drunk every day. (A good alcoholic rationalization.) The drugs Fran was taking to combat the symptoms of schizophrenia and paranoia made him tired and uncommunicative. He seemed to be doing well at work, but at home, he was always in another world. He would fall asleep shortly after dinner, get up early go to work, come home, eat, fall asleep, etc. day after day. We never went anywhere or did anything as a family, and I lived in constant fear that he would never get better.

In 1976, we transferred back to St. Louis. We were tired of apartments and found a home that was perfect for us. We moved into our new house on December 17, 1976. It was a new development and our house was one of the displays. It seemed so big after living in apartments and the boys were so excited. We didn't have to "shush" them anymore; they could run and scream all they wanted. As families moved in there were more and more kids to play with, and the boys were happy and healthy. Our third son, Tim, was born on October 7 1977, the same day my paternal grandmother died. I was so sad about her death, but so elated to have a new baby at home. Trey and Mark were thrilled to have a new baby brother, and things were looking up. We seemed to have weathered the worst where Fran was concerned. We bought a speedboat and spent every weekend on the river. The boys loved the water, and for the first time in years, I felt all was well. Wrong again.

Fran began having problems again and his temper was out of control. He would fly off in a rage about nothing, and accuse me of having affairs. He hated to take the drugs as they made him feel awful, but it was apparent that without the drugs he could not function. He started seeing another psychiatrist, but he was getting worse. All I could think of was "Oh, no, not again." It seemed that one more time my life was whirling out of control, and I began drinking more. At this point, I would drink beer, scotch, vodka, and bourbon, but never gin. It smelled too much like my Dad. I honestly thought I was a good mother since I never really hit my boys hard, (another alcoholic rationalization), but emotionally I was not there for them. I can't imagine how awful it was for them with their Dad yelling crazy stuff and me drunk on my ass. To quote a fellow member of the program "… the message my kids got from me was 'Yes, I love you; now go away.' They had to be practically invisible in their own home. I had absolutely nothing to give them emotionally. All they wanted was my love and attention, and alcoholism robbed me of the ability to give it. I was empty on the inside."

At one point, Fran's psychiatrist wanted to see me. I remember the doctor asking me if I drank. I said "Yes" and waited for him to lecture me about my drinking. He said, "I don't blame you." Not what I expected, but it sure gave me the go ahead to continue drinking since he obviously didn't think that was a problem. He also said something that stuck with me for years, "Get out of this marriage as fast as you can, before it is too late." It was not long after this that the doctor sent a letter saying that he was dropping Fran as a patient and never wanted to see him again. Apparently, Fran had gotten very abusive in the doctor's office.

Fran started seeing another doctor and was hospitalized again for a short time. In the summer of 1978, Fran, the boys, and I went to Florida where Mom and Dad had rented a condominium. Fran was acting weird again and was certain we were all out to get him. (In a way, he was right, my Dad wanted to kill him.) Needless to say, the trip was a disaster and I had to watch him constantly so he would not hurt anyone or do something stupid. I was at the point where if he wanted to take his life fine, do it, just don't take us with you. I had asked for help from the doctors who had seen Fran. I begged them to please put him in the hospital and keep him there. I told them he had threatened suicide and wanted to kill me, but they said they could not help me unless he did something to hurt me. The police said the same thing. When I begged his parents to help me get him hospitalized, they refused, insisting I was blowing everything out of proportion. I was in the pit of despair and could find no way out. Every where I turned no one could help me. My descent into hell was accelerated when I had a miscarriage. I was drunk and fell while water skiing. I should never have been skiing, and the guilt of killing an unborn child was devastating to me. Thus started a two-year binge where I seldom breathed a sober breath, and the committee in my head never ran out of coffee. It was non-stop: "You killed an unborn child." "You don't deserve to live." "How could you do such a thing?" "You have made a mess of your life." "You should be ashamed."

I have often said that God put alcohol in my life to keep me alive. Alcohol made everything better. Life was livable when I was drinking. Life was manageable when I was drinking. I began to drink around the clock. My mornings would start at 6:00 AM with a mason jar full of wine. In fact, I had a mason jar full of wine in every room of the house in case I could not get to the kitchen. After the boys left for school, I spent my mornings driving around town to stock up on beer, scotch, or wine. Towards the end, it was all wine. I could not afford anything else. I would buy those big wine jugs with the round loop on top; white wine $2.99 a bottle, what a deal. I would drive to the ends of the earth to get my wine. I never went to the same store twice in one week. I was afraid they might think I had a problem. Dumping those jugs when empty became a challenge. I would never put them in the trash; they made too much noise when the garbage men threw them in the truck. After I gathered the empty bottles, (if I remembered where I hid them), Tim and I would throw them in dumpsters, empty fields, other people's trash cans. If it were beer or scotch bottles I would toss the empties into the blue post office boxes around town. Making sure I had enough to drink was the most important thing in my life. Saturdays were the worst, as I had to make sure I had enough to get me through Sunday, since we could not buy liquor on Sundays. Most days when the boys came home from school, they would find me passed out or drunk. I even locked the front door sometimes so they could not get in and bother me or interfere with my drinking. I found Tim asleep in the front yard one afternoon, he had on a pamper and cowboy boots. Did I really think this was normal? I was usually drunk, when Fran was beating on Trey, or Mark. I was not there to stop the abuse, and this is the hardest truth to swallow. These little guys had no one to defend them, and I will be eternally sorry that this happened. The boys dinner, (if they even got dinner), was always hotdogs, Ding Dongs, and dry cereal. I don't remember Fran ever hitting Tim, I guess because he was only one or two years old.

I was a stumbling, pissed off, ugly drunk, and I didn't give a damn about anybody anymore. I embarrassed my family, my Mom, and my Dad. I passed out in restaurants, I passed out playing monopoly one evening and jammed a hotel through my forehead, (it's ok to laugh!), I even threw up in my purse in the backseat of a car, thinking no one would notice. I fell down the steps in a fancy Chicago restaurant; I was escorted out of a restaurant and carried to the parking lot—still sitting in the chair. I just went through the motions of daily survival and each day was the same; drink in the morning, drink all afternoon, make something for dinner, drink, go to bed, get up at 2:00AM to drink some more, get up at 4:00AM to drink, get up at 6:00AM and do it all over again. Someone once said that alcoholics are cowards. As far as I am concerned, alcoholics are some of the bravest people I know. It's hard work being an alcoholic. It takes guts to get up and do the same stuff over and over again. I embarrassed the boys at school, I drove drunk carpooling, and I would stagger out to get the mail. I was always mad at Fran. It was all his fault. I hated him for screwing up our lives and I hated me for staying with him and not having the guts to leave. I hated God for allowing this to happen. Alcohol was taking me places I didn't want to go and I could not stop. I could not envision going through one day without alcohol.

# 10

## *The Courage To Change*

Several times after Fran and I would have a fight I would go next door to complain to my neighbor. She finally had enough one evening and called Mom. Mom came over, screamed at me calling me an alcoholic, and said she would take the boys away if I didn't stop drinking. Neighbors had approached me about my drinking and I just shrugged it off. I later found out that they were so concerned about the boys that they were thinking about calling the police. Fran starting confronting me about my drinking and I would scream at him and tell him it was all his fault, that I hated him and wished he were dead. One time he said he wished he was dead too, and I prayed "Please make it happen." What an awful time this was for the boys. All the emotional, verbal, and physical abuse going on. Fran would push me and slam me against walls, calling me awful names and yelling about how terrible a mother I was. He was out of control and I desperately needed help. I agreed to meet with an alcohol and substance abuse counselor. She said that I needed to go into rehab and I absolutely refused to go. No way, no how. I honestly felt that I could not stay sober being locked away for a month, and then thrown back into the same environment. If I was to get sober and stay sober, I had to be at home doing the daily things I was supposed to do, not in a cocoon protected from life's problems. There was also no way I would leave the boys with Fran for a month. I didn't trust him to take care of the boys (as if I was the perfect mother.) If I was going to stop drinking, I had to do it my way.

I don't know what happened that morning. I was starting my day as I always did with one difference: instead of pouring wine in a mason jar, I poured the wine down the kitchen sink. After the boys left for school, I called a gal down the street who went to meetings. I agreed to go to a meeting with her the following Wednesday, Sept. 23, 1980. I stayed dry the week before the meeting and have not had a drink since. What a miracle! Sobriety has been tough, a lot of stumbles along the way, no wine, but a lot of whine.

Onc of the most bewildering symptoms of alcoholism is denial. When I walked into my first meeting, I weighed about 92lbs. I was gray and bloated, shaking so badly I could not hold but an inch of coffee in a cup. I had the dry heaves but insisted I didn't have a problem with alcohol. I sat and didn't hear a word that was said, as I was too busy noticing that I had nothing in common with these women. When I left one of the women said "You will never make it without treatment." I stayed sober another week and another week, and then a month and another month just to show her I didn't need treatment. I went to one meeting a week for a year and amazingly I stayed sober, but for all the wrong reasons. I came late to meetings and left early as I had no desire to be friends with these women. If the word "God" or "spirituality" was the topic of a meeting I left. I was so angry at God I just didn't want to hear about a "Higher Power."

The situation at home was worse, not better. I assumed that if I went to meetings and didn't drink everything would work out. I was so wrong. Fran was becoming increasingly abusive to the boys and me, and I found myself afraid of him. He was not supportive of my getting sober. It's like the line I heard at a meeting: The wife says, "I liked you better when you were drinking." And the husband says "I liked *you* better when I was drinking!" I would have to get my Mom or a babysitter to come to the house when I went to meetings.

One of the hardest things for a recovering alcoholic is finding something to take the place of drinking. When King Alcohol rules your life, and the King is taken away, what do you do? Drink coffee—lots and lots of coffee, and nurse those resentments. When active, every thinking moment is devoted to alcohol, "Do I have enough." "I need to get more wine so I don't run out." "I have to carpool today, so I have to be careful." Do I have enough money to buy more alcohol." "Where should I dump the empty bottles today." I had to do something to keep busy, to help me stop thinking about drinking. I decided to plant tulips. I ordered five hundred bulbs and planted every one of them. The following Spring the tulips came up, and there were tulips everywhere! People slowed down and pointed as they drove by the house. The tulips were all different colors and they were beautiful. Most of the tulips came up again in the following years, but none as pretty as the first season.

When tulip season was over, I decided to bake pies. I don't even like pie that much, but decided it was something I could try. I'm a very literal person. The first time I made brownies the box said mix by hand, and that's exactly what I did. I had my hands in the bowl of brownie mix when my Mom came in and she was howling with laughter. One more time I proved to her that I really am an idiot. Anyway, the pies must have weighed ten pounds each. I obviously mis-read something in the recipe. I didn't last long baking pies. No one would eat them.

I was determined that my first sober Christmas was going to be a great time for the boys, so I decided to decorate the shrubs outside with stings of lights. I had six strings, one hundred lights per string, and tested them all before I began stringing them in the shrubs. About half way through, I decided to turn them on to see how they looked. One string was not working, so I had to unplug that string from the one that was working, and test each light to see where the problem was. Having fixed that, I started again. Knowing the first two strings worked, I added two more strings, and turned the lights on again. Now the second string was not working. I unplugged the second string and fixed the light. Now I had four strings working, and decided to test the last two before stringing them. They worked, so I attached them to the strings that were already on the tree. Done! I turned them on and none of them worked. So, I unwound all of them to find the one light that was not working. I found the problem, they were all working, and I strung them again. I flipped the switch to turn them on and nothing happened. None of the lights worked. So, I unstrung them from the shrubs, and laid each string the length of the driveway. I then proceeded to stomp the hell out of every one of them. I calmly swept it all up, and threw all but one string in the trash. The one I saved I put in the trunk of my car to remind me of how angry I can get.

After six months of going to the Wednesday night meeting, I made the decision to stop attending as nothing was changing for the better. I arrived at this decision about 7:00 PM on a Wednesday evening. Within a minute after deciding this, a lightening bolt came through the ceiling, a big blue ball lit up the kitchen, there was a roar of thunder, and the power went out. I went to the telephone, called the fire department, and then a babysitter, and got my ass to the meeting. I have been going ever since. I am afraid not to! To me, the lightening was a wake up call to get my act together and get serious about this twelve-step program. It is funny, but when I decided to change my attitude, things began to come together. I starting attending additional meetings, and at one meeting I heard my story. This woman talked about a Sunday afternoon when she was in the kitchen with her three little boys and one of her kids knocked her vodka bottle off the table. She immediately grabbed a sponge to absorb the vodka and wrung the sponge over a glass. I had no doubt that I would have done the same thing, and I knew at that moment I was an alcoholic, and if she could stay sober so could I. The amazing thing was at that moment I *wanted* to be sober!

I knew that for this program to work I was going to have to become willing to accept a Higher Power at work in my life. Since the God of my childhood was not working in my adulthood, I had to open my mind to a new God of my understanding. I began to believe as a result of watching how others lives had changed for the better. I heard them talk about "Turning it over" living "One day at a time" and "Keeping it simple." I made a decision to work the steps; I made the decision to work towards that personality change sufficient to bring about recovery from alcoholism. I wanted what these women in Group 166, my homegroup, had; I wanted to be happy, joyous, and free.

As a result of making that decision, I began to realize that I could not continue in my marriage. Fran refused to take his medicine or keep his doctor's appointments. We had taken a trip to Michigan the summer of 1981, and I was just miserable. We fought the whole time and I could not wait to get home. Fran was very agitated most of the time and his grabbing, swinging, and shoving the boys and I was getting out of hand. I contacted an attorney and made the decision to file for divorce. The next two years were a living hell. I went through three attorneys until I found one who would take my case. Since there was no precedent for granting a divorce from a paranoid schizophrenic, finding a lawyer to help me was tough. Although Fran agreed to move out and got an apartment close by, he would come to the house, just walk in, and refuse to go home. He would not leave us alone. He would come over at night and throw rocks at the windows demanding I open the door. One evening he got angry because I would not let him in, and he broke the window in the kitchen door and tried to force his way in. He took off when he heard me call 911, and as expected, the police didn't do a thing. One of the most frightening events was when I happened to look out my bedroom window at around 3:00 in the morning, and he was standing there in the yard staring at me. I went to court for orders of protection and restraining orders to keep him away. They were worthless. When Fran violated them and I called the police, the police would do nothing. A couple times, he was picked up for trespassing, but was always released a couple hours later. Because it was obvious that Fran had mental problems the police were lenient with him and totally disregarded the havoc he was causing. Until he seriously hurt the boys or me, the police would do nothing. Ridiculous. The boys knew they were not to let him in the house and if he was prowling around the neighborhood, they were to come home immediately. Fran had threatened to take the boys away from me, and I knew he would if he had the chance. During one of the many court hearings, I was granted temporary custody. He was furious, tried to get the boys from the school playground a couple times, but the faculty was advised of the situation, and they called the police.

While all this was going on, I began cleaning houses to earn some money. Amazingly, Fran still had his job, and the court ordered him to give me one-half of his paycheck for expenses but it was not enough. My lawyer had told me that I would need to show the judge I could support the boys and myself, or he would most likely order Fran and I to sell the house. I could not let that happen. These boys had been through so much; losing their home was not an option. I was determined to stay sober and be a better mom. However, the boys were somewhat uncomfortable with their new sober Mom. I found Mark crying one day and when I asked him what was wrong he said, "You don't love me anymore." I asked him why he thought that and he said, "Because you don't yell at me anymore." How sad. How could I ever make it up to these kids?

I had tried many times, unsuccessfully, to get Fran committed. None of the doctors would help, saying he was not a threat to himself, or anyone else, and that paranoid schizophrenics were not normally violent people. What? One day, after we had come home from shopping, Tim came running up the stairs to say that Fran was downstairs on the floor and not moving. Of course, the first thing I thought was that he had finally committed suicide, after all the threats he had made. I was again furious that he had gotten inside while we were gone, so I went flying down the steps. Fran was on the floor and unconscious. I could not wake him up and I called 911. The paramedics shot him full of epinephrine and they could not rouse him. His heartbeat was very shallow and his pulse was almost nonexistent. They rushed him to St. Luke's Hospital and I followed the ambulance. After waiting forever a doctor told me that they could not wake him up and that he was in a catatonic state. Fran was transferred to another hospital with a psych ward. They wanted to admit him, but I refused to sign the involuntary commitment papers. I was not going to be responsible for payment. Fran's parents came to the hospital, just furious with me, but his father signed the papers. As was usually the case, Fran was released after a short period of time, and it all started again. He lived with his parents for a short time, and then got another apartment close to us. He had started seeing a doctor again and was taking his medicine.

It was in the middle of all this craziness that my Dad came to the house one afternoon. I heard something crashing outside and when I opened the front door, Dad was throwing the boys' bikes all over the driveway. He was in a rage as he staggered up the steps to the door. In a very calm voice he said, "I just came by to tell you that you're the biggest disappointment of my life." I honestly don't remember what my response was, or if I even had one. I knew he was drunk, and my committee said "He didn't mean it", but my heart was crying. Dad never mentioned it nor did I, but I carried that hurt for years.

# 11

## *The Strength To Go On*

Fran lost his job, and that meant no insurance for the boys, and no child support. His company had been supportive of him, and would have kept him on but he would not stay on the medicine. He would begin to feel better and then stop taking the drugs. It was at this time that my Dad's secretary retired and I asked if I could step in. Dad said great, so I had a decent paying job and insurance. Things were starting to look up when Fran's car died and he took mine. My name was not on the title so the car was legally his. Mom and Dad bought me a used Dodge Omni, and I still laugh every time I think of that car. I had a friend at the corner Amoco station and he would pass my car at inspection time, knowing I could not afford to have any work done on it. After three years of doing this, he finally said he could not pass it again, and would feel responsible if something happened to me and the kids while driving that car. I tried to keep the car clean and did get the oil changed occasionally, but one time I decided to have the engine cleaned, thinking it might run better if all the gunk was cleaned off. I still remember standing there watching the engine being cleaned and nuts and bolts and all kinds of "thingys" falling out. The guy who was doing the cleaning was horrified, and didn't charge me. Apparently, the parts were not terribly important as the Omni kept on running. When it was finally time to get rid of it for safety sake, it would not go into reverse or park and the emergency brake didn't work. During this time, Fran had bought a sporty Honda convertible and would swing by to show it off to the boys. One night I got a call from him. He was in New York City. He had driven there, sold the Honda, and needed a way home. I told him to call his Dad.

Although the divorce hearing was put on the docket several times, the lawyers would file a continuance since Fran was either in the hospital or off his drugs and/or incompetent. My lawyer didn't want this divorce granted when Fran was sick, as it could be overturned. Fran retained an attorney who told him since his name was still on the house he could legally move back in, and he did. To me, this was the worst thing that could have happened. For approximately six months, Fran was living in the house. He slept in the living room, never spoke to the kids or me. I didn't cook for him or wash his clothes. It was an awful situation and when I look back on it now, I don't know how I did it. God just gave me the strength to keep going and to trust it would all work out in the end. The shoving, pushing, and verbal abuse started again. One morning I was in the kitchen cooking breakfast. I had just cooked bacon in a skillet, and when I turned around, Fran had the skillet by the handle and was getting ready to toss the hot grease over me. Mark jumped up between Fran and I, and was able to reason with Fran to put the skillet down. I knew then that I could not turn my back on him or trust him. I was so mad at his blaming me for his illness that one evening I threw a handful of mashed potatoes at him. God that felt so good! Mea Culpa. He would corner me in a room and ask who I was and where Dana went. He would get so angry when he could not find me, and scream my name and make threats. It was getting to be too much for me to deal with. I was wreck. I was afraid for my life and afraid of him hurting the boys. The committee in my head was raging, and I started to hear "You could stab him while he's sleeping." "No one would blame you." "You could say it was self-defense." "They wouldn't arrest you." "The police have been at the house so many times they would probably be glad it was over." I was coming apart, and the committee was scaring me. My attorney went to court and filed a petition to have Fran removed from the home. He was given several days to leave and of course he refused. He left when the police showed up and he went to his parent's home.

He then began calling at least fifteen times a day. He harassed by way of telephone calls, and coming to the house and beating on the doors. More orders of protection were filed, but again, the police felt sorry for him and would not arrest him. Fran decided to fight the divorce and seek full custody of the boys. Since Missouri is no fault there was nothing he could do about the divorce, and there was no way I would agree to joint custody of the boys. He decided to represent himself at the initial hearing and the judge ordered him out of court and not to return until he had an attorney. Fran did all he could to paint me as a bad mother including telling the court I was an alcoholic. Fran had made such a fool of himself in front of the judge in earlier hearings that my attorney told me not to worry there was no way the judge would agree to joint custody. During early negotiations, I had requested that Fran sign a quick claim deed and I agreed to give him $18,000.00 when I sold the house. I asked for child support and no alimony. He was told to pay two hundred and seventy-seven dollars a month total for all three boys. Gee, thanks judge! Fran was also responsible for one-half of the boys medical insurance and one-half of all their medical expenses. I had to agree that Fran could have the boys on alternate weekends. I absolutely hated agreeing to this and to the one day a week visitation. On March 17, 1983, the divorce was granted. I wanted to stop at a bar to celebrate, but when I called home, my sponsor answered the telephone and told me to come straight home. She knew exactly what I was thinking.

# 12

## *Hello*

It was finally over. The boys and I could move on. Boy was I wrong. All hell broke loose. Fran was on a constant rampage and would not leave us alone. His periods of illness were more frequent and the holidays were always the worst. His parents were still in denial about his illness and would have nothing to do with me. On one occasion, the boys had gone over to spend the weekend at Fran's parent's home. Mark called and said that I needed to come and get them as everybody was fighting and they were scared. I immediately left to get the boys, and told Fran and his parents that these boys would never be visiting them again. There were times when I would not allow the boys to spend the weekend alone with Fran. If he was not taking his meds, the boys would not go, period. I received letters from Fran's attorney that I was breaking the law and in violation of a court order. I didn't care. My boys were not going to be with Fran if he could not be trusted. The boys didn't want to go most of the time, and I never forced them to go. As far as I was concerned, Trey (12) and Mark (9) were old enough to make up their own minds about spending time with their Dad. Tim (6) would not go alone nor would I let him go alone. I felt I was the only one who could determine if it was safe for the boys to be with Fran, not the court, and not his attorney. Fran took me back to court on one occasion to say he should be allowed to move in with us because he owned half the house. He never told his attorney about the quit claim deed. When I showed up in court with the deed the case was dismissed. So was Fran by his attorney.

Fran continued the constant badgering by telephone and by showing up at the house, and then he started writing letters about how I was doomed to hell if I didn't change my ways. This went on for five years after the divorce. I would continue to call the police and they would do nothing, or Fran would take off before they arrived. I had been to the courthouse to see if there was anything more I could do to keep him away. Another brick wall. There was nothing more my attorney could do. I just couldn't believe no one could help me.

One afternoon the telephone rang and it was the assistant district attorney from the county. She said that my file had ended up on her desk, and she asked what on earth was going on. The file showed all the calls to the county police, 911 calls, violated orders of protection, trespassing charges, abuse charges, restraining orders that were issued, and she was shocked that nothing had been done to stop this. There is no way to express how I felt when I got that telephone call. Someone was finally going to listen and hopefully stop Fran from making our lives so miserable. She said she was going to look into this and gave me her telephone number. The next time there was any trouble, Fran was to be charged and jailed. I found out that Fran had numerous charges against him filed by other people, and he had begun hassling the police department. He was picked up for vagrancy, disturbing the peace, loitering, trespassing, and other miscellaneous charges. This lady was my angel. She was all I had hoped and prayed for, and she gave me her word that this would stop.

Things started to calm down. Fran was hospitalized for an extended period at the city mental hospital, released, and was living on the streets. He could be seen walking and hitchhiking along the highway and on busy secondary roads close to our home. He never came by but would hang around the corner for a while until the police told him to leave. I would see him around the stores where I worked, and he would sit and wait in the parking lot where my dentist was, hoping to catch me going in for an appointment. We began to get on with our lives. He would still send letters to me and the boys and call occasionally to talk with the boys, but no major problems, until one day he called me making absolutely no sense and raging about turning me into gazelle meat. (You can't make these things up!) I recorded the conversation and went to the police that evening. The stalker law had just been passed a few months before so I was confident that they would arrest him. I also brought a file of all the arrests and problems we had experienced to prove that we had been stalked for years. The policeman just nodded his head and said there wasn't anything he could do since Fran had not physically harmed us in any way. My God, not that again! I just lost it. I told the policeman what I thought and I slowly spelled my name and wrote it on a piece of paper so he would remember me when he saw the headlines that my ex-husband had killed me. I was beyond angry. Nothing had changed.

However, something had changed. Fran just up and disappeared. It was wonderful. We had our life back. We assumed he was in the hospital. Months went by without a word. Mark got in touch with the social worker to see if he knew where Fran was and if he was OK. The social worker said he was living at a church operated shelter, and doing odd jobs. Even after all we had been through, we were glad he was doing as well as could be expected. I was at the point of just feeling sorry for him. Through the twelve steps and praying for him each night, the resentments I had toward him dissolved. I was able to stay sober and with the help of my new God, my sober friends, my sponsor and my meetings, I never had the desire to drink. And I am so grateful. I began to develop a healthy relationship with my boys, although I did play the part of "Supermom" until I wore myself out. They had been through so much and I wanted to make it up to them. What kind of an amend could I possibly make to these boys? I was told to make an amend of consistency, and that is what I did. Life was good.

My sponsor passed away in July of 1984. She was the only person I had ever been honest with, and I missed her terribly. The boys and I would go to her house to visit a lot as she had the cutest pugs Tong and Chong. She would baby-sit for me so I could go to additional meetings and the boys really liked her. I had met her husband, Bob, at the grocery store once and he seemed nice. He was an attorney for a retail chain and traveled a lot. Their four kids all lived away from St. Louis, and when Helen died I wrote Bob a note, and told him if there was anything I could do to please call. Several weeks later he called and I met him for a hamburger. I will never forget what he had on—a striped shirt and checkered pants. He looked like an orphan and I told him to never wear that combination again. We talked and he seemed sad and lost. He said he and Helen had just closed on a lake house and he was probably going to put the house back on the market.

Bob called a couple weeks later and invited the boys and me to the lake for a weekend. I remember we could only go on Sunday as the boys had soccer games. We had a wonderful time and I encouraged Bob to hold on to the lake house, as he may enjoy it more than he thought, and his kids could come down for long weekends. Well we began spending as much time as we could at the lake house and Bob bought a boat so we could ski and fish. The boys were in heaven and it was so great to see them having such a good time. Bob began to help me with the carpooling to soccer, and would stay for dinner. He gave me Helen's car to drive and I sold the Dodge Omni. He also started helping me financially and wanted nothing in return. I felt funny taking money from him but he insisted. He was irate at how Fran had treated us and he just wanted to help. I knew he was getting serious and wanted this to be more than a friendship and I got scared. I told him I could not see him anymore and that I was not willing to give up my freedom. The boys and I were happy with our lives and there was no way I would jeopardize what I had worked so hard for. He was crushed but he promised not to push, and to give me all the room I needed. He had been going to Alanon for about sixteen years and stopped going several years earlier. He decided to go back to meetings and with both of us working twelve step programs we grew closer. He asked me to marry him in 1986, but I said no. I was just afraid of getting hurt again. He never mentioned it again until the spring of 1987 when he asked me again because he needed a tax deduction. He was serious and I thought that was hysterical. I said yes, and we were married July 17, 1987 at St. Vincent De Paul Church. My parents and the boys were the only ones there as we didn't want anything fancy. We put an addition on the house (a master bedroom) instead of moving to a larger home.

I had applied for a church annulment in 1985. In retrospect, I think I filed only to prove to Fran's parents that I was not at fault for the problems in the marriage. They were devout Catholics and no one had ever gotten a divorce in their family. Fran was contacted by the Church regarding the annulment, and he was livid that I was applying for an annulment and he wrote the Archdiocese, the Tribunal, and the Pope (honest) to protest. My annulment was granted in six months, which was amazing. It usually took two years to get one. I was glad I had done it after I agreed to marry Bob so we could be married in the Catholic Church. Well, I could not find a priest who would marry us. I was told that although I had an annulment, I was still divorced and therefore could not be married in the church. What? I contacted a priest whom I had met at one of my meetings. He had left the church and suggested I call Father Tom at St. Vincent De Paul in downtown St. Louis. He said the priests there were not under the thumb of the Archdiocese. I called Father Tom and he said of course he would marry us. I was already angry with our local Parish and this just did it. Why bother with an annulment? Several years before a representative from the local church came to the house requesting a donation towards the building of a new church. I told them I was financially unable to do this, and he told me that I was not welcome in the church if I could not contribute. I realized again, that my God was present at my meetings and in the people who kept me sober. My new God was not concerned about how much money I could give the church.

The boys were not very excited about us marrying. They liked Bob, but he could be rough around the edges at times, and I would become very defensive if he came down on the boys. It was an adjustment for all of us but before long, "The Bobster" was accepted and things ran smooth. For awhile.

# 13

## *Goodbye*

In 1988 and 1989 we had twenty-two hospital visits, some resulting in admission to the hospital. We had a broken arm (Tim trying to do an Ozzie Smith back flip), several broken fingers (Mark, Trey, me), two broken legs (both Mark), a broken hand (Trey), two broken noses (Mark), knee surgery (Bob), cervical disc surgery (me), broken collar bone (Mark), dislocated shoulder (Mark), rehab (Mark), two dislocated knees (Tim, Mark), and numerous ER visits for x-rays, stitches, and physical therapy. Welcome to my world! One evening we all went up to the corner to have a pizza. It was quite a sight to see: Bob was limping from his knee surgery, Mark and Tim were both on crutches, Trey had a cast on, and I had a neck support on. People were holding doors for us, helping us in and out of the car, and trying not to laugh. Bob had retired, thank God, as now he had a full time job taking care of us!

Trey left for Mizzou and partied the year away. When he was home for the summer, he received a letter from the University not inviting him back. Trey was shocked and could not believe it. I remember him asking me "Can they do that?" He then started at the Junior College that September and went two years. Trey was anxious to get out on his own and moved to an apartment. He had odd jobs, but finally got a decent job at a car dealership. Tim was doing very well in school despite having short-term memory problems. Mark on the other hand was heading towards disaster. Mark is dyslexic and he had a terrible time in school. He hated it because he could not keep up with the work. When he started high school all he talked about was playing first string on the varsity soccer team. He had to maintain decent grades to play, so our hope was that high school would be the turn around for him. The first varsity tournament game of the year Mark broke his leg. It sounded like a gun had gone off on the playing field. The ambulance came and we went to the hospital. You could just see the pain in his eyes, not necessarily the pain of the leg, but the pain of all his plans and dreams disintegrating. Six months later, the doctor gave him the OK to play soccer, and Mark broke the leg again. No more soccer—ever.

We lost Mark to drugs and alcohol that year. His disappointment and anger took hold of him. We requested that he be enrolled at the new alternative school in the district. Mark needed affirmation that he was not a failure, and we hoped the school would help his self-confidence. He did well at the start, but decided that drugs were the answer to all his problems, and I could certainly relate to that. I confronted him several times on his drug use, but he always denied he was using. He started stealing money from us, lying and gone all the time. He and Trey got into a fight one evening and Mark ran off. He ended up in the emergency room and I was called. The doctor talked to me about Mark's using and he arranged for Mark to go into treatment directly from the hospital. Mark was livid, and hated me for doing this. He even called a social worker and claimed he was abused by Bob and I. I only saw Mark a couple times when he was in treatment and when he was released he came home and said he was going to meetings. I wanted so badly to believe this that I gave him the benefit of the doubt, but he started skipping school, quit his job, and started hanging around with kids I didn't know. I gave Mark the ultimatum: stop using, find a job and go to school or leave. Mark said he wanted to go to treatment again, and I said no way. The answers he needed were at the meetings, and we could not afford to send him again. One afternoon I found some drug paraphernalia in his trunk. I issued no more threats, I told him he had to leave. It was one of the hardest things I have ever had to do. I can still see him draining his waterbed, and throwing stuff out the bedroom window. Someone I didn't know picked him up, and I felt so bad, I could not stop crying. We didn't hear from Mark for some time. The Principal at the school called to say Mark was back in school, and would I please reconsider letting him come home. I said "No", Mark and I had a deal and he could not hold up his end. Mark was told what would happen and until he straightened himself out, he was not welcome at home. Tim came in one day in tears to tell me that Mark was eating out of the dumpster behind Dunkin Donuts and living in the woods, would I please let him come home. I said no, and it just broke my heart to stay firm with my decision.

I was at the lake house one weekend when Bob called to tell me he had just bailed Mark out of jail. When I got home, I found out that Mark had tickets for a DWI, careless and reckless driving, trying to leave the scene of an accident twice and destruction of public and private property. All this had happened at 7:30 in the morning! Thank god we had put the car title in Mark's name so no one could sue us. Mark was in a heap of trouble and knew it. He got an attorney and went to court. I went to the hearing and sat in the back praying. My heart just stopped when the judge said he was going to put Mark away for two years. I don't know what Mark's lawyer said to the judge, but Mark was given a suspended sentence for two years, had to call in weekly to a drug counselor, pay some hefty fines, and serve many hours of community service. If he was picked up for drinking or drugging, he would go to jail for two years. His license was suspended for six months, and when he was able to drive again his insurance cost him 3200.00 for six months. Did he learn his lesson? Yes, thank god, he did. We told Mark he could move back home but the rules had not changed. Mark graduated from high school, and got a job cleaning cages in the research department at a local university. He attended meetings, made new friends, and made the decision to stay sober, one day at a time. Mark moved into an apartment with a friend he met in the program and I was beside myself with joy. Tough love had worked with Mark, and I was so grateful.

My Dad asked Trey to come in to the business to help with sales. Dad had a product he was trying to sell, and was leaving the railroad supply sales to my brother and Trey. Trey was a very good salesman. I always said he could get anybody to buy anything, as they would buy whatever it was he was selling just to get him to shut up and stop talking! Dad was eventually going to move the business to Kansas City where my brother lived, so Trey moved to that office. He was doing a good job selling and brought several good accounts into the business. I got a call from Trey one morning and he told me he had been picked up on a DWI the night before and the company car had been impounded. I had to go to Kansas City to get the car out of hock since I was an officer of the company. I knew Trey drank, and he had a couple alcohol-related incidences in college, but this was the first time he had gotten into any real trouble. He was remorseful and embarrassed about what he had done. He retained an attorney, paid the fines, and was able to keep his license, as it was a first offense. When business began slowing and the money stopped coming in, Trey went to work for another company. Trey knew his salary and benefits were hurting the company and he took the job to reduce expenses for Dad. I was still working part time at the business, but my Mom had started doing the secretarial work and I only went in a couple times a week. Trey was transferred to Houston, TX. and seemed to really like his job. He was making great money, had a new SUV as a company car, and seemed to have found his niche. He was dating a girl and seemed to be settling down. Trey had been on his own ever since he was 18, and I was proud of him and of what he had accomplished. Because he lived away from home for several years, I had no idea he was in serious trouble with alcohol.

In 1988 and 1989 Bob had a couple scares with his heart, but the problem was treatable through medication. However, in the spring of 1992, Bob had to have vascular surgery as an aneurysm showed up on a routine x-ray. It was a very serious surgery, but he came through it fine. Poor Bob was like a walking scar. He was pretty beat up in World War II, and had a huge scar down the inside of his thigh and leg. Tim would bring his friends in to see Bob's scars and his Purple Heart. In October of 1993, my dear friend Phyllis died after battling leukemia for six months. She was only fifty years old and one of the funniest people I ever met. She was loved by all of us at Group 166, and her death left a scent of sadness for months to come. In the spring of 1994 Bob was having some vision and balance problems. He had a check up and all was well, so we were not unduly concerned. On April 1 he fell on the stairs and could not get up. Tim called me at work and I rushed home. We took Bob to the corner "Doc-in-the-Box" and were told to take him to the ER at St. John's Hospital. They did a CT Scan and the doctor came in and told us that Bob had an inoperable brain tumor. I was beyond shock. Bob's comment was "I can't complain, I've had a great life". Unbelievable. Bob was admitted to the hospital, and he began radiation treatments. He was transferred to a skilled nursing facility and went to the hospital everyday for tests. I could not bring him home yet as he could not walk, but I knew I had to get him out of that place. It was depressing and smelled. It was obvious Bob was getting worse, but we brought him home in hopes that he would get better. I gave him shots of heparin in his stomach every day, but I realized he was going to need more care than I could give him. One day when I was taking him to the hospital for a radiation treatment, he fell in the driveway and I could not get him up. I called 911 and they took him to the hospital. He was admitted and I was told there was nothing more they could do. I talked to his family and they agreed he needed twenty-four care. I found an opening at Rosewood Hospital and it turned out to be a wonderful place. The staff was very caring, and Bob was happy there. He was failing fast both mentally and physically, but I was so grateful he was never in any pain. The day before he died he asked me if I saw the man in the white robe sitting in the chair. I do not remember what my response was, but Bob said, "He asked me if I was ready to go and I told him not yet." I received a call the following afternoon, about ten minutes after I had left Rosewood. Bob's nurse said to come back as he was having trouble breathing. I raced back and stayed with him until he died the following morning, June 4, 1994. It was a beautiful day and there was such peace in the room when he passed. We had a beautiful service at the funeral home and I found a Unitarian pastor to speak, as Bob was a Unitarian before he was an Alanoner. I used to tease Bob about all his girlfriends in Alanon, and they were all at the wake to tell him goodbye. I asked his kids to come to the house when convenient to retrieve any furniture or family items they wanted. I didn't feel right keeping stuff that had been in Bob's family for years. I still keep in touch with Bob's son Ralph. The other three kids never warmed up to me, and that is fine. It really was not about me anyway; they just didn't want to share their Dad after their Mom died.

Bob loved the hummingbirds that visited the flowers on our deck, and he would sit and watch them every evening. A couple days after the funeral I was sitting on the deck crying and a hummer flew up to me. It fluttered six inches in front of my face, and stayed there for ten seconds and flew away. To me this was Bob's way of saying "I'm still here, and everything will be fine." Shortly after, I had a hummingbird tattooed on my ankle.

# 14

## *A Time To Mourn and a Time To Dance*

Tim and I lived in the house for another two years, just until Tim could finish high school. Trey and Mark were on their own and doing fine. The boys were all so supportive after Bob died, and I know they missed him just as much as I did. As Mark says, "He was the only Dad we knew." In the summer of 1996, I decided to sell the house and move into a condominium. The house was just too much for me to keep up; the yard itself took an entire weekend. We planned the move while Fran was in the hospital so there was no way he could trace us, and we asked the new owners to please not tell anyone where we had moved. It was very hard on Tim to leave the only house he ever lived in, but he knew it was important to me. Before I sold the house, I called my attorney regarding the payment of the $18,000.00 the court ordered paid to Fran upon my selling. I had kept records of all money received from Fran, and he was behind $22,577.00 in child support, medical insurance, and medical expenses. My attorney said that since I had proof, I didn't have to give him the money, and we would go back to court if necessary. The subject never came up, and apparently this payment was never recorded, as it was not flagged in the title search. I have never looked back, or regretted selling. I also sold the lake house, and there are days when I wish I had kept it. The gals and I had many fun weekends at the lake, but I could not afford the upkeep of two homes. Tim moved into an apartment with one of his friends and I was living alone for the first time in my life and loving it. I have never experienced the "empty nest" syndrome.

Tim decided to go into the Army, and moved back in for a couple months before he left. I still remember the day he left. As we waited for his ride to come, I could tell he was nervous and second guessing his decision. I encouraged him all I could without crying, but when he gave me a hug and walked out the door, I just started sobbing. He was stationed at Ft. Benning, GA. and wanted to go into the 82$^{nd}$ Airborne as a paratrooper. That decision caused me many, many sleepless nights. He would call every couple of weeks, and when he started jumping out of planes, I was a basket case. I turned that one over to God. When Tim came home on leave, he looked great. He had put on weight and seemed to really like what he was doing. He was sent to Egypt for several months where he broke his collarbone (bike riding). The army didn't do anything about the break, and it healed badly, and he broke it again. They then operated and pinned it, and Tim was able to come home for two weeks after the surgery.

At 2:30AM, the day Tim was to return to Ft. Bragg, I got a call from an ER nurse at St. John's Hospital. One of those calls parents hope they will never have to answer. The nurse said Tim had been injured in an auto accident and I needed to come to the hospital right away and bring some-one with me. It was June 4, 2000; the same day Bob had died six years before. I remember getting on my knees and asking God to please help me accept His will. When I got to the hospital, the trauma doctor and nurse were at the door waiting for me. I asked if Tim was alive and they said "Yes", but he was in critical condition. He was in the ICU and on a venti-lator. He had eight broken ribs, a punctured lung, a gash on his head, and other smaller injuries. I asked if Tim had been driving and the doctor said no, that the driver had been killed instantly. I can still remember the panic I felt when he said this, as I knew Mark was with Tim. I asked if the driver's name was Mark and he said no, but he could not tell me who the driver was. I knew it was one of Tim's friends and the thought of one of those boys being killed was awful. Mark and Em, (Mark's wife to be), came in after me as they had gotten a call from one of Tim's friends about the accident. Mark said the boys had been out drinking and he had called a cab to take them all home. Apparently, after they went back to one boy's home, they took Tim's car for a ride. They knew the driver was Steve. I had not met Steve although I knew the name.

We went to the ICU to see Tim, and since most of his serious injuries were internal, he looked much better than I expected. The doctor asked that we not tell him about Steve right now, and that was so hard to do as Tim kept asking us if he was all right. We told Tim that Steve was at a different hospital, and we had not gotten a report yet on how he was doing. The ICU waiting room was full of my friends, Tim and Steve's friends, and Mark's friends. Tim didn't remember the accident but he did remember pulling Steve from the car and starting CPR. The paramedics said they had to pull Tim off Steve, and he was hysterical, not comprehending that Steve was dead. They almost lost Tim on the way to the hospital. They had to put a tube in his chest to drain the blood and it was touch and go for a couple of days. Trey had flown in and we were so glad to see him and he stayed with Tim around the clock. Finally, we had to tell Tim that Steve had died. I think he knew but needed someone to say it aloud. Tim was devastated and cried and cried. It just broke our hearts. He blamed himself for Steve's death and since he has an EMT license, he thought he should have been able to save Steve. He was consumed with survivor's guilt. Tim's doctor told him "If I had been on the corner with all my trauma staff ready when the crash happened, I would not have been able to save Steve." That seemed to give Tim some comfort. Tim was released from the hospital after five days, and the one person that helped him the most was Steve's wife Sue. In spite of her grief, she was by his side throughout this terrible time and her caring made it easier on all of us.

Tim stayed with me an additional month, and then he needed to return to Ft. Bragg. One of the hardest things for Tim was not remembering the accident, and he was afraid that maybe he was the one driving, not Steve. The police began an investigation to determine the cause of the accident, and who was driving. The car was demolished and it was very hard to figure out what had happened. The police determined the car was going eighty miles an hour when it hit a concrete wall and there were no skid marks. They said they had never seen a car this totaled where someone lived. I saw the car and I just could not believe what I was seeing. The police were not convinced that Steve had been driving and that really scared us. We got an attorney, and waiting for that determination as to who was driving was agonizing. If Tim had been driving, and was responsible for Steve's death, I think it would have destroyed him. A witness had said that Steve was driving, but that was not good enough for the police. It took months before they were convinced Steve was driving. The proof was the imprints of Steve's shoes on the pedals. When the medical examiner's report was released, it clearly stated that Steve's injuries were indicative of his being the driver and I felt the weight of the world was lifted off our shoulders. Sue is still a close friend of Tim's and I am so grateful that she never blamed Tim for the accident. Both Steve and Tim had been drinking, and one more time, alcohol was involved when something bad happened. My heart broke for Steve's parents, and what I didn't know, was soon the heartbreak would be mine.

On September 29, 2000 Mark and Emily were married. I was so excited and so happy for both of them. I absolutely adore Em and her family. They had decided to have a Celtic wedding and they did all the planning and arranging. It was incredible. The wedding was at St. Vincent De Paul Church, the same church Bob and I were married in, the same church Em's parents were wed, and the same priest that officiated at her parents wedding performed the ceremony. It was the most beautiful wedding I could ever have imagined. The bagpiper played and Mark and I walked down the aisle together. He was dressed in a kilt of McLean plaid, and the ceremony was performed according to Scottish tradition including binding their hands in the plaid, and pinning a sash of plaid on Em's dress. The whole family was involved in some way, and the guests said it was the best and most beautiful wedding they had ever attended. I was so proud of Mark, he had overcome so much, (I need to mention that a couple years before, Mark legally changed his name to Mark Dana McLean). Tim was unable to attend, but Trey was in the wedding and looked so handsome. The day was perfect, absolutely perfect. I would not have changed a thing, except to have Tim there. He was unable to attend because of his service commitment, but was with us in heart. The reception was on the top floor of a downtown building with a beautiful view of the city. Mark and Em settled into a cute little house in South St. Louis, and all was good.

I had been talking to Trey more often, and he would come home a couple times a year. He was still in Houston and seemed serious about a girl. He brought her home for Thanksgiving in 2000 and although we were not that crazy about her, we were willing to accept her if she was Trey's choice. The following spring they were having problems, and Trey was about to lose his job. He told me that the company president was in legal trouble, and they were cutting back on sales agents and he was in line to be let go. He was also in credit card trouble and I bailed him out of that on the condition that he come home. I just had a feeling this girlfriend was nothing but trouble. She was going into rehab for the third time and she had two children that Trey just loved (he was always so good with kids), but they lived with her Mom. She didn't work and was hanging around with some questionable people. Trey did lose his job, and he moved back home with Katie the cat. When Tim came home from the Army, Trey gave up the bedroom for Tim and moved into the unfinished side of the basement. Everything was going quite well. Trey was busy looking for a job, and found one in auto part sales. He was good at it but hated the job. He was gone from six a.m. to ten p.m. every day, and when he came home, he was up doing reports half the night. He left that job which was fine with me. I didn't like seeing him so miserable. He then went to work for a friend of his he had known since they were five years old. It was a roofing company, and was a part time job for Chuck, but business was so good he wanted to go full time in the future. He asked Trey to help run the business, give estimates, hire workers, etc. and Trey loved what he was doing, and he began looking for an apartment. In the meantime, Tim was at lose ends and Chuck asked him to come work for him. Both boys had jobs they liked and it seemed things were going well for them.

It had been mentioned to a friend of mine that her husband, who was in the same business as Trey used to be, said Trey had a drinking problem and that's why he was fired from the Houston job. I was very surprised when she said this and angry. Trey had been living with me for almost a year and I had no indication that he was in trouble with alcohol. He would occasionally buy a six pack of beer, but it would stay in the refrigerator for a week or more before Trey finished it. He went out in the evenings, and most times, he came home while I was still up. We read, watched movies, and hung around in the evenings. There were only a couple instances where it appeared he had drank too much, but he always had a ride home. He knew how I felt about drinking and driving. Since Trey had moved out when he was eighteen, I was glad to have this time with him. We were alike in so many ways, particularly liking the same movies and books. Katie the cat made herself at home and my cat, Holly the snot, was not happy to have Katie around but they learned to tolerate each other.

# 15

## *Sorry For Everything*

On the morning of Monday, July 1, 2002 as I was leaving for work, I noticed that Trey had not come home the night before. I was not particularly concerned, as he would sometimes stay at a friend's house. Tim had already gone to work and I saw the rental agreement on the kitchen table. He and Tim had decided to get an apartment together, and had begun filling out the form. I was working at a local office supply store, and I got a call around 11:30AM from the police. A neighbor had called the police to report someone breaking in the back door. The police said when they were checking the inside of the house they found a man downstairs unconscious, and the description fit Trey. I left work and when I got home there was an ambulance at the house, and the paramedics were downstairs. When I came in I immediately went downstairs and the paramedics were performing CPR. They asked me if I knew of any drugs he may have taken and I said no; thinking that he probably had too much to drink the night before and was just passed out. As they took him out on a stretcher I held his hand and told him I loved him. One of the policemen said that he had left a note. It said "Sorry for everything call Cardinal Towing for car Bye."

The police officer asked me if I thought, as they did, that this was a suicide note. I just went cold. Suicide had not even entered my mind, and I said "No"—instant denial. On the way to the hospital, the seriousness of this began to settle on me. When I arrived at the hospital, I was taken to a room and a priest was waiting. I was told the doctors were with Trey doing everything they could. What did that mean? Was he going to die? What was going on? A doctor came in the room and asked if I knew what Trey had taken. They were convinced that he had taken too many pills of something. I again said I had no idea what he may have taken. I called Tim and

Mark to tell them what was going on, and if they knew of any drug Trey may have overdosed on and they said "No." It seemed like I waited forever. When another doctor came in I remember looking at him and saying "He's dead isn't he." The doctor nodded his head and said, "I'm so sorry, we were not able to save him." My friend, Ann, Mark, and Tim came in moments later. That afternoon Mark told me that Trey had been picked up a couple times on a DWI in Texas. Mark was aware of the alcohol problem and thought I knew. I wish I had known, maybe, just maybe, it would have made a difference. The committee in my head tortured me for months, "You should have known he was an alcoholic." "You should have paid more attention." "This is all your fault because you were drunk all the time when he was growing up." "You never protected him from Fran's abuse." "If you had found the empty bottle of pills earlier, he may have lived." "You should have never told him to leave Theresa and move back home." "You should have been more interested in what was going on in his life." I'm sure that any parents, who lose a child to suicide, blame themselves, and this guilt consumes every waking moment. Although my guilt has, for the most part, subsided, the committee in my head still voices these opinions, usually when I'm hungry, angry, lonely, or tired.

I believe God gives us an anesthetic when these things happen, to help us get through the days ahead. When the boys and I went in to see Trey, he looked like he was sleeping. I could tell that he had died soon after he arrived at the hospital, as his skin was cool. We cried, said a prayer, kissed him, and said goodbye. It was so very hard to leave him. As we were leaving the hospital, we had to make a decision on how to tell my parents. Mark and Tim said they would drive over to their house and tell them. I do not remember going home; what I remember next is my home filling up with my friends. I then remember Dad walking in with the boys behind him, and then Mom came in. She ran to me sobbing, and asking why did he have to die, why did God not take her instead of Trey. She was so upset and could not accept that Trey had taken his life. Trey was her first grandchild, and I knew a flood of memories was rushing through her head. True to form though, Mom and I went outside and she asked me to please not say he had committed suicide in the obituary and I told her that

I would not lie about how Trey died. The boys and I had agreed that we would not put Trey's death notice in the paper for fear of Fran showing up, as Trey absolutely hated his Dad. We also put a lawyer's address on the birth certificate so Fran could not trace our whereabouts. We spent most of the afternoon calling family and friends. Ann made most of the calls for me, as I was just not up for explaining everything.

From what we could piece together, Trey had been picked up on a DWI. They towed his car, and he spent the night in jail. He walked home, and knowing how angry I would be, he decided to take his life. I think there were other events in his life that contributed to his decision, as he had mentioned to one of his friends that he was "tired of pimping off of everyone else's life." It was not until that night that we found the empty bottle of pills. The medical examiner's office called and wanted to know if I knew what he had taken. Again, I said "No" and was asked if he may have taken any of my pills. I went to the medicine cabinet and found the empty bottle. I had just filled the prescription the day before. I was so upset that I had not looked before I left for the hospital. I just never thought about my pills. I then went through the "if onlys" but the medical examiner said it would not have made any difference, since he took so many pills and they were so fast acting. I just could not forgive myself for not remembering my pills, and it was not until I talked to Dr. H. my shrink, that I finally accepted that it would not have changed the outcome. Dr. H. lost his son in a car accident last year, and we talk about our emotions in dealing with the loss of a child. My regular doctor also lost his daughter to suicide a year after Trey died.

Mark, Tim, and Sherry, Tim's girlfriend, all stayed with me the night of Trey's death. Emily was eight months pregnant and we encouraged her to go home and get some rest. We camped out in the living room and laughed, cried and shared our sorrow. The following morning we all went to a meeting. This is what we do now instead of drinking. We go to a meeting and share our sorrow with the people who love us and support us. Grief in sobriety is a very hard emotion to get a handle on. We used to drink to take the pain away, but now we learn to face the bad with courage, dignity, and faith. After the meeting, we all went to the funeral home to make arrangements. We decided to have a wake the next evening, July 3, with an open casket, and then Trey would be cremated. Picking out a casket for the wake was very hard on all of us. They kept playing that Josh Groban song "You Raise Me Up" and I could not stop crying. We also picked out a box for Trey's ashes and three silver teardrop pendants with Trey's ashes inside. We wanted everyone to come to the house after the wake, although because of the July 4th holiday, we didn't expect a big crowd. Ann took care of the flowers, and the gals took care of all the food and preparation. I do not know what I would have done without my Group 166 women, my sponsor, and my new friend, Nettie. My heart will always be full of gratitude to these women who supported and helped me during this tragic time.

The wake was to be from 4:00 PM to 8:00 PM on July 3. The funeral home was a long drive for many people, and the traffic was terrible because of the holiday. The funeral director had told us that Trey's was the only wake scheduled so we were free to roam without disturbing anyone. All of the sudden the place started filling up with all these people. Someone said there was no place to park and cars were parking in the adjacent cemetery. There were people there I didn't even know, but they were friends of Bill W. and they were there to offer support. People were standing in the hallways and the three rooms we had requested were full. There was love and there was laughter. That's the way it is when Bill's family is together. Mark read a beautiful eulogy he had written for Trey, and we all said goodbye one more time. Mom seemed to hold up fairly well, but Dad was beaten. He kept saying, "I should have done more for the boy," (Dad also had a committee in his head). I tried to console him but he continued to blame himself for Trey's death until the day he died. I wanted to say, "Dad you are not that powerful," but he would have never understood. When we were leaving, the funeral director said they counted over 350 people and it was the biggest wake they ever held. We were so grateful all these friends came to pay their respects. As we turned into my subdivision, I said that someone must be having a party, as there were cars parked all over the place. It was only when we reached the crest of the hill that we realized all these cars belonged to people who had come to visit after the wake. My mouth just dropped, and I remember saying "We don't have enough food!" Well, it was kind of like the loaves and the fishes, all of a sudden there was plenty of food. I was in tears. I was so touched by the people who stayed to be with us. I made new friends, and met many neighbors who brought food and hugs. It was a beautiful end to a sad, sad day. When we picked up Trey's ashes, we went to the cemetery where Bob was buried, and sprinkled the ashes over Bob's grave. I remember we all said something as we scattered the ashes and we all cried and said goodbye again, and forever. A couple weeks later, the committee in my head said, "Trey's ashes are just laying on top of Bob's grave." "You can't just leave them there for people to walk on." I went to the cemetery, and on my hands and knees, I picked up every fragment I could find, and I put them in my God box.

I went back to work a week later. It was probably too soon but I didn't know what else to do. I still had a life to live. The grief of losing a child is beyond description. Your heart literally aches, and I felt I was bleeding to death inside. I ordered a couple books from Amazon that were about losing a child, but I could not find one that talked about the death of a child as a result of suicide. I read and read to see how others got through the dog days after death, but nothing seemed to help. I then decided to go to a suicide survivor meeting at the hospital where Trey died. I cried through most of it, and didn't find the answer there either. I went to three more survivor meetings and never went back. I listened to parents talk about their son, or daughter, and how they didn't celebrate birthdays or holidays any more; how they shut the door to their child's room and never went back in again; and how they left all items as they were when their child died and have never moved a thing. These people were not living, they were merely existing. I wanted more; my life was not over. One more time, I found the solution: go to meetings, call your sponsor, read the Big Book, work the steps, live one day at a time, forget the shouldas, wouldas and couldas, be grateful, and carry the message. Works every time.

Emily was pregnant when Trey died, and we were so concerned about the stress on her and the baby. She seemed to be feeling fine, and we were all so excited about this baby, my first grandchild. We all headed to the hospital when Mark gave us the call we were waiting for. It seemed to take forever! We did have a lot of fun in the waiting room, betting on the time, the sex, hair/no hair, color of hair, etc. It was good to laugh and we even had the other families joining in the fun. We were able to go in and see Em until it got rough and then we waited. The doctor decided on a cesarean and Mark said he would let us know as soon as he could. It felt like we waited hours, and Em's Mom and I were getting worried. We then heard Mark in the hall "It's a boy!" I was just beside myself with joy that it was a boy. I hugged Mark and just cried. It was like all the stress of the past couple months came pouring out of my eyes. They named him Gavin Trey McLean, and he was born on August 16, 2002, forty-five days after Trey's death. He was beautiful and healthy. Every time I look in his eyes, I see Trey. He is a sweetheart and could not have been born at a better time for all of us. His birth was a gift, and Trey lives on in the eyes of his nephew.

# 16

## *I Will Always Love You*

In November 2002, Mom broke her hip. She had surgery, which went well, but her blood pressure dropped, mucous was filling her lungs, and they needed our permission to insert a breathing tube. Of course, we said yes, and they took Mom to ICU. It was touch and go, and I stayed with Mom in ICU and held her hand all night. I was so afraid of losing her. It was a long, long recovery for Mom. She developed "Thrush," a painful rash in the mouth and throat. She was unable to eat and was wasting away. She was so dejected, saying she was never going home. On Christmas, we all went to the hospital to be with Mom. She looked awful and was so weak, but was able to see and hold Gavin. I noticed Dad was losing weight even though I was cooking meals for him to take home, as he would never cook for himself. He also would not eat what anyone else cooked, and he had no idea how to do the wash. Mom had spoiled him rotten. He swore he was eating, but each day I could see that he was going downhill. He was lost without Mom. They had been together since he was seventeen, and could not function without her. Mom finally seemed to rally, and she was on a walker and doing well. She wanted to go home, and her coming home was the best Christmas present we could ever get. She started baking cookies and was on the road to recovery. Of course, she started waiting on Dad hand and foot, and all was back to normal. However, I knew it wasn't going to be normal ever again.

In February 2003, Dad finally went to the doctor, and was diagnosed with lung cancer. We were kind of expecting that because of the weight loss and terrible cough he had. He started radiation treatments, and Mom took him to the hospital three times a week. I would leave work and meet them there, watching as they walked, holding each other up. There was no apparent change in Dad's condition, and the radiation had the same effect on Dad as it did on Bob—none. We all realized that it was a no win situation. We stopped the treatment, and brought Dad home to die. Mom had promised Dad that she would not put him in a nursing home, so my brother and I spent as much time as we could with her and Dad. Dad tried to rally a couple times, even ate a little now and then, and never lost his sense of humor, but we knew it would be soon. We finally called Hospice and arranged for a bed at home. Dad lasted a week, and it was a horrible death to watch. Because Dad was an alcoholic, his resistance to drugs was so high that the normal dosage didn't do a thing. He was not in pain, but his anxiety, and inability to sleep, was wearing on all of us. We had to talk to the doctor, the nurse, the hospice representative, and the pharmacist to get his dosage changed, but by that time he had stopped fighting, and wanted to die. You just kind of know when someone is ready to go. He fell into a deep sleep, and seemed at peace. There was no struggle, just a sigh and he was gone. Oh, the tears. First Trey, now Dad. Mom was so tired from all the care she had given Dad, never leaving his side, and I was so concerned about her health. Mom had decided on cremation for Dad, and when they came to take him away Mom just fell apart. How my heart ached for her. Dad died on June 12, 2003. Mom wanted to wait to make plans for the wake, as she had an appointment to keep.

When Mom was in the hospital with her hip, the doctors saw something on her lung, but decided to follow up on it later as they knew the situation with Dad. Mom made an appointment for the first week in July and I took her to see the same respiratory doctor she had while in the hospital. He explained that the malignant tumor in her lung was operable, and they would just take out the lobe. The surgery sounded awful to me, and I wanted to tell Mom to not have it done. I asked the doctor if she was a good candidate for this type of surgery, and he assured me that she would be fine. Mom was 82 years old, and I was just not convinced this was a good idea. It was her decision to do it, in spite of my concerns. The surgery went fine, but Mom was in terrible pain and the morphine was not helping. When my brother came in to see her, she said "Oh, Papa, you came!" She thought it was Dad. She then went to sleep and everything went downhill. Her lungs started to fill with fluid, and they put her on a ventilator. The last thing she said to me was "I'm never going to get out of here." She was right. She went to sleep, and never woke up. She was in ICU, and we kept looking at the x-rays of her lungs, but each day there was no improvement. Rose, my wonderful ex-sister-in-law, came in from Kansas City to be with my brother and I. Rose was like a daughter to Mom and is still a sister to me. It was an agonizing week for all of us. There was no improvement with Mom, and it came time for us to make a decision. We talked to the doctor, and he said that if Mom did pull through, she would have to live with a tracheotomy, be on oxygen, and confined to a wheel chair. In addition, it appeared there might have been brain damage. It was not a hard decision to make; we needed to let her go. I could never look Mom in the face if I allowed her to live under those conditions. She would hate me for letting it happen. One of the doctors was furious about our decision, and threatened to take action against us. He said we just didn't want to take care of her, and left the room. I could not believe it. I was so angry, what a terrible thing to say to a family. What we were doing was carrying out her wishes. The staff in the ICU were very embarrassed about the doctor's outburst, and said as far as they were concerned, we had made the right decision. We went to speak to the doctor who did Mom's surgery, explained what we wanted done, and he was in agreement with us, and felt it was the best. Then we waited. We stayed with Mom in ICU the rest of the day and into the night. She was never alone. We talked, and we laughed at the stories Mom and Dad used to tell us. Just in case Mom could hear us, we made sure we told the one's she liked. Mom died the following morning, and one more time, tears, grief, and goodbye. It was July 25, 2003. Mom also wanted to be cremated so I picked up hers and Dad's ashes at the same time, and had them mixed together in the urn we had bought for Trey's ashes. The obituary in the paper announced their deaths, and that there was going to be a celebration of their life at their Parish Church, with a reception following at the club-house where Mom and Dad lived. The service was short and well attended. The priest knew Mom and Dad, so it was a personal service, and we were all invited to say something if we wished. The neighbors talked about how every morning Dad would deliver everyone's paper; how funny Dad was in his various hats; how Mom and Dad took care of the flowers in front of the building; how they helped bring in groceries for residents, and how much they were going to miss Mom and Dad. Mom had asked me years ago to have someone play Debussy's song *Clair de lune* at her service, and we found a piano player who knew the song. Not a dry eye in the place. What a wonderful tribute to Mom and Dad, I hope they were as proud as we were. We scattered their ashes at the edge of the trees where Mom and Dad would watch the deer, coyotes, and raccoons. It was hard getting their condominium ready to sell, so many memories, and two big problems. First, we could not find Mom's will. Thankfully, their attorney had copies. Second, Mom and Dad had started the paperwork to apply for a reverse mortgage. Part of this process was removing me as the beneficiary on the deed. I did not know this, and when I sold their condominium, I got a call from the realtor saying that the condominium wasn't mine to sell. I couldn't believe it. Again, the attorney stepped in and took care of the paperwork to have me declared the beneficiary so we could proceed with the sale of the condo. It took weeks to get this straightened out, but the buyers were great and understood the situation. The distribution of Mom and Dad's belongings went fine; absolutely no arguments over whom got what. Ralph, Rose, and the granddaughters, Julie and Kate, came in from Kansas City to help Mark and Tim load the furniture. We laughed when no one wanted the yellow velvet chairs the kids were never allowed to sit on. Before the chairs were carted out, Tim said to wait, there was something he had always wanted to do. He started jumping up and down on the chairs (with shoes on) and Kate joined in. Sorry Mom.

# 17

## *Today*

I miss my Mom and Dad and some days it's like being an orphan. Although my Dad was an alcoholic, and Mom his biggest enabler, they loved each other very much and went through so much together. They supported me in all my decisions later in life, and were my cheering section when I chose sobriety. I caused them so much pain when I was drinking, but they accepted my amends and never stopped loving me. I have come to realize that they did the best they could, and they always wanted what they thought was the best for my brother and I. The resentments I had towards them disappeared long ago and I know today, that I was blessed to have such loving parents. Mom and Dad never hugged us when we were growing up, but when I introduced them to hugging they made up for lost time. They were so pleased whenever the boys would come over and give them hugs. Mom and Dad adored the boys, and I know my boys will always have wonderful and fun memories of "Maw" and "Paw."

Mark has been sober now eleven years. What a gift to have him in recovery. He is an honest and decent human being, who loves his family and knows what is important in life. I am so proud of him. Mark and Em added a girl to the family on May 11, 2004. Maison Elizabeth McLean (Maisie). I thank God every day that I had boys. Maisie is a piece of work. Mark says she sucks the brains right out of him. She is the drama queen of the family, and has her Dad's sense of humor. We are hoping to stop the spread of the disease of alcoholism with this generation, but we are a little concerned since one of Gavin's first words was "more." We took a family vacation to Frisco, CO. in the summer of 2004; we saw the Garden of the Gods, and Manitu Springs, and the magic of the mountains will always be with me. It was so much fun showing the kids all the places I loved as a child.

In the fall of 2004, Tim, who was in the reserves, was called to help fight the war on terrorism. Before he went to Kuwait and then on to Iraq, he and Sherry were married at Ft. Bliss. When he left, I remember thinking "I don't know if I can do this." There is this fear of losing another child, and I can't go there. It was tough when Tim was gone, but I had to remember it was tougher on Sherry. I stopped reading the paper and listening to the news. What saved me from going nuts was email. What a wonderful thing for those of us who have loved ones in harms way. Of course, the days without an email were almost unbearable. Sherry and I were both working, but managed to see each other at least once a week. Sherry's mood was always up, and she was so supportive and proud of Tim as we all were. There was one instance when after several days without an email, my imagination took off and I was a basket case. Tim finally called and I will never forget what he said, "If something happens to me, I want you to know, that I can't think of a more honorable way to die than serving my country." I knew then that he would be just fine, and I swelled with pride. Sherry was pregnant, and the baby was due in July 2005. We were expecting a girl and we were so excited. Sherry even found a home for them in South St. Louis, so all would be ready for the baby, and for Tim when he came home. Mark had painted the baby's room pink, and there were pink ruffles, pink blankets, pink clothes, and even a pink cradle in the front yard. Tim had the OK to come home for the birth of his baby girl, and the doctor induced Sherry when Tim arrived home. I was in the delivery room and it was an incredible experience. When that baby popped out we couldn't believe it. It was a boy! The doctor was so surprised and we all just started laughing. All I could think of was the song "A Boy Named Sue." Chase McLean Nolan entered our world on July 13, 2005. Mark repainted the walls blue, and a neighbor repainted the cradle in the front yard. Tim had to go back to Iraq the end of the week, and that goodbye at the airport just about did me in. Tim came home for good in November, 2005. I was amazed at how one week Tim is dodging bullets and the next week he is changing diapers. Sherry and Tim just had another baby boy, Nicholas Calvin Nolan, on Sept. 30 of this year. Another gift we accept with open arms.

The heartache of Trey's death is with me every day. I have thirty years of memories of my son. It took me almost two weeks to write Chapter 15 as the tears still flow freely, and at times, the grief is worse than the day he died. The last thing he said to me was, "I love you", and my last words to him were, "I love you too." That was the night before he took his life. I take comfort from my first Mother's Day without him. I was on the porch crying and as I looked up there was the biggest and brightest double rainbow I have ever seen. Thank you Trey.

Sad to say, my brother and I are not close. We are four years apart, and when growing up, we were just involved with different things. Mom and Dad's death hit him very hard, as Dad was his best friend. He had a heart attack this year, and I went to Kansas City to help him out, but he is uncomfortable being vulnerable. He always insists he is fine, even when I know he is not. He is just not "into" family and I have to accept that our relationship, or lack of, is the way it is, like it or not. I love him very much and I hope he finds happiness. His ex-wife Rose is like a sister to me, and he has the most wonderful daughters, Julie and Kate, and two beautiful grandchildren.

Fran lives in St. Louis, and I have had no contact with him for over ten years. Tim occasionally speaks to him. He lives on disability and is apparently taking his medication. According to Tim, when told about Trey's death, Fran said Trey had that "look in his eye," whatever that means, and he then asked Tim for money. It took me a while to let go of the resentment I had for Fran. I started to pray for him, as the program suggests, and amazingly it worked, the resentment faded away. I made my amends to Fran, which I never thought I could do, unfortunately he thought I was apologizing because I wanted us to get back together. I still don't think he gets it.

My life today is quiet in comparison with the past. I had lived with chaos for so long that at first it was hard to get used to serenity. I lost my job at the office supply store because I chose to be with a friend who had a heart attack and emergency bypass surgery, and I was late calling work.

Actually, I was glad, as I was not happy there, and one more time God did for me what I could not do for myself. At present, I am a bookkeeper for an animal hospital, and I work part time as a cashier at The Home Depot. I love to read and draw, and have even designed several tattoos for friends. Since I need to work, I don't see my family as often as I would like, but I hope the day will come when I can spend more time with them.

I have had many little miracles, some call them coincidences, since I made the decision to turn my will and my life over to a Higher Power. One of the most memorable happened several years ago. I still felt guilt over the miscarriage years ago, and although I knew God had forgiven me, I could not forgive myself. My friends and I went out to dinner one evening and someone asked me if I had a little girl what would I name her? I had always thought that the baby I lost was my little girl, and after reflecting on that for a moment, I answered "Mariah." Months later when Tim was leaving to go overseas, he bought me an angel to go with my Seraphim Classic Collection. It is a porcelain angel with her arms extended towards heaven, and she is holding a baby wrapped in a pink blanket. I turned it over to read the inscription on the bottom and it said, "Mariah Heavenly Joy." Tim knew nothing of my conversation over dinner, and when I explained the meaning of it to him, I believe the word he used was "spooky." I finally felt forgiven.

God and my meetings are the priorities in my life today. If I don't maintain my sobriety I will again lead a life of quiet desperation, and I refuse to live like that again. I never planned to be an alcoholic, but I thank God every day that I am. I have so much fun and I have the most wonderful friends in the world. I have traveled to Seattle, San Diego, Toronto, Las Vegas, Florida, and Montana. I know that it's no big deal, people travel all the time, but for someone who panics at the thought of getting on a plane, it is a big deal. My dream has always been to see New York City. In May 2001, my friend Ann and I went to The Big Apple. What a thrill! My eyes just welled up with tears when I saw the skyline and the Statue of Liberty. We stayed in Times Square, rode the subway, hailed a cab, rode a sight-seeing bus, went to the theatre, shopped in the jewelry district, and walked Fifth Avenue. Four months later the Twin Towers were hit, and I felt such a deep sadness for the city and the people who lost their lives. I hope to go back again soon to continue the tour. In 1998, I was diagnosed with depression and I also sponsor women with the same illness. Medication allows us to work our program to the best of our ability. There are many in the fellowship that are anti-medication and I support that position up to a point. I feel lay people should not interfere with a legitimate diagnosis from a psychiatrist well versed in the disease of alcoholism, as is my doctor. Some members have the same attitude regarding medication for depression as the public had about alcoholism years ago—denial of the disease and the mistaken assumption that willpower is all that's needed. Our rigidity can kill us if not checked. Because I have an understanding sponsor who has walked beside me all the way, I have not found it necessary to take a drink since September 17, 1980, and for that, I am eternally grateful. Watching the women I sponsor grow, and in turn carry the message, is one of my greatest joys. I try to live each day with so much gratitude that I can't imagine living it any other way. I have surrendered and am living life on life's terms. The committee in my head has adjourned—temporarily.

978-0-595-41306-5
0-595-41306-4

Printed in the United States
68079LVS00004B/608